AN ILLUSTRATED GUIDE TO THE
ISRAELI
AIR FORCE

AN ILLUSTRATED GUIDE TO THE

ISRAELI

AIR FORCE

Bill Gunston

a Salamander book

Published by Arco Publishing, Inc.
NEW YORK

A Salamander Book

Published by
Arco Publishing, Inc.,
219 Park Avenue South,
New York,
N.Y. 10003,
United States of America.

© 1982 by Salamander Books Ltd.,
27 Old Gloucester Street,
London WC1N 3AF,
United Kingdom.

Library of Congress catalog card
number 81-71938

ISBN 0-668-05506-5

All correspondence concerning the
content of this volume should be
addressed to Salamander Books Ltd.

Contents

Credits

Author: Bill Gunston, former Technical Editor of *Flight International*, Assistant Compiler of *Jane's All the World's Aircraft*, contributor to many Salamander illustrated reference books.

Editor: Philip de Ste. Croix
Designer: Mark Holt
Three-view drawings:
© Pilot Press Ltd. and
© Salamander Books Ltd.

Color profiles: © Pilot Press Ltd., and © Salamander Books Ltd.

Printed in Belgium by Henri Proost et Cie.

Acknowledgments

When I began to write this book I soon realized how little information was readily available. Israel has always been as tight on security as any nation on Earth, and there is practically nothing on the official published record. I am particularly indebted to *The Israeli Air Force Story* by Murray Rubinstein and Richard Goldman. Arnold Sherman of IAI has told the story of that extraordinary company in *Lightning in the Skies*. Stephen Peltz, one of the few Westerners to have been conducted, with camera, round Chel Ha'Avir bases, very kindly read the text of this book, and supplied many of the excellent photographs we have included. A special mention should also be made of Yehuda Borovik, publisher and editor of *BIAF — Israel Aviation & Space Magazine*, who acted as consultant on the text of the book and also provided a host of photographs. I would like to express my gratitude to everyone else who supplied photographs: the IDF Spokesman, Tel Aviv; the Embassy of Israel, London; Danny Shalom of Bavir-Aviation Publications; Lt-Col David Eshel of Eshel-Dramit Ltd; J. G. Moore; IAI Ltd; and Tadiran.

Bill Gunston

Introduction

This book is about the aircraft of the air force of Israel. Israel is one of the world's smallest countries, but its armed forces are large, well-equipped and perhaps the most skilled and professional in the world. This is the natural consequence of history. The birth of Israel and of its armed forces is a story without parallel.

The land at the eastern end of the Mediterranean has had many names and rulers, and as chequered and turbulent a history as any place on Earth. From 1516 it was ruled — after a fashion — by the Turks. In 1917 Britain's General Allenby conquered the country and its existence was formalized as Palestine, about the size of England's Hampshire, Sussex, Surrey and Kent combined, or one of the small New England states in the USA. Under British mandate peace reigned, even though the population comprised two totally dissimilar groups: the Arabs and the Jews.

For several not very good reasons Britain tended to support the Arabs, and from 1939 prohibited Jewish immigration to Palestine. Though Arab attacks on Jewish life and property were a daily occurrence, Palestine Jews were forbidden to have weapons. World War 2 was merely a temporary diversion which among other things filled the land with Allied war materiél and several airbases. After 1945 Britain could not get out fast enough, and the UN in its wisdom decided to partition the country. A large chunk in the East was given to the new

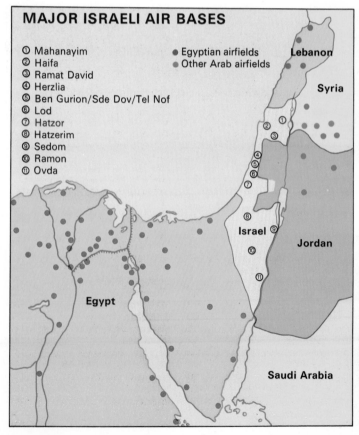

MAJOR ISRAELI AIR BASES

① Mahanayim
② Haifa
③ Ramat David
④ Herzlia
⑤ Ben Gurion/Sde Dov/Tel Nof
⑥ Lod
⑦ Hatzor
⑧ Hatzerim
⑨ Sedom
⑩ Ramon
⑪ Ovda

● Egyptian airfields
● Other Arab airfields

Lebanon
Syria
Egypt
Israel
Jordan
Saudi Arabia

Arab state of Jordan. An even larger region in the South (today called the Sinai) was given to the Arab kingdom of Egypt, together with an important fortified coastal zone called the Gaza strip. What was left was a tiny area for the Jewish population called Israel.

To state that the Arabs — all Arabs — resented the creation of this small Jewish state would be a gross understatement. Even before the Union Jack was lowered for the last time at sunset on 14 May 1948 armed raids on Jewish settlements had gradually merged into open warfare; but the Jews were strictly forbidden to have any defences. With the most extreme difficulty a clandestine Sherut Avir (aviation service) was built up using the handful of mostly prewar lightplanes that the British allowed to be in Jewish hands.

At midnight on 14/15 May Israel, which had just come into existence, was invaded on all fronts by forces of Egypt, the Lebanon, Syria and Jordan (the British-trained Arab Legion), with further contingents from more distant Iraq, the Sudan, Saudi Arabia and even Morocco. The Arabs were determined to destroy Israel before it could acquire any proper weapons and armed forces. That the Jewish state survived is nothing short of a miracle. The Sherut Avir had a mere handful of beaten-up light aircraft to operate against squadrons of Spitfires, Furies, Hurricanes, Fiat G.55s and many other Arab warplanes.

What followed is one of the true epic stories of modern times. For the first year the situation was desperate. Even after Israel had become a sovereign state, and formed an air force — the Chel Ha'Avir — on 27 May 1948, almost all of the world's countries refused

Above: VQ-PAM was an RWD.13 and VQ-PAR the Dragon Rapide *Aaron*; date 25 October 1947.

Below: In the early days the Israelis kept going by getting spares from shot-down Egyptian Spitfires.

to supply it with arms. While individual Britons and Americans, and sympathizers (by no means all Jewish) from many other countries, flocked to join the Chel Ha'Avir, their governments maintained a strict embargo on all forms of arms sales to enable the new state to drive out its invaders. The inevitable result was an amazing underground activity which sought aircraft for airlines and even air forces that did not exist, scoured dumps of junked aircraft for anything useful, met suspicious characters prepared to do anything for a roll of banknotes, set up phoney film-making companies to create epics involving wartime aircraft, and by every conceivable means constructed an air force in the hardest possible way.

Modern air staffs who spend ten years doodling around a single requirement might find it difficult to comprehend a situation in which an air force grabbed eagerly at anything that would fly. In most cases the next stage was to knock together gun mountings and bomb racks from any bits of pipe and angle that might be to hand. Britain had pretended to be in the same situation in the summer of 1940, and is proud of the idea of Tiger Moths with bomb racks. Curiously when Israel was in even more desperate straits eight years later the official British view was cold disinterest, though substantial arms deals were concluded with all the surrounding Arab countries.

Two of the most often-told stories of those crucial first weeks describe the acquisition of the first Israeli fighters and bombers — as distinct from lightplanes trying to act like fighters and bombers. Unquestionably, they were the worst fighters and bombers (relative to

Above: In the tough early days the Harvard (as all T-6s were known) was a front-line aircraft.

Below: The survivors, and later additions, were repainted and served as trainers throughout the 1950s.

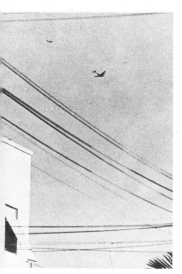

Above: Spit after Heinkel? No, an S 199 on the tail of a C-47 that had bombed Tel Aviv!

Below: Unquestionably, the S 199 was more dangerous to its friends than to any of its many enemies.

the technology of the day) in all history. The bombers had at least once been properly designed B-17s, but they had been totally de-militarized in a singularly crude manner. They were not exactly flying wrecks, and had been in-tended to fly cargo in South America, but their turrets had been replaced by unbelievably ill-fitting pieces of aluminium and plywood held on by non-aeronautical bolts and even pieces of wire, and all navigational devices had been re-moved, other than drift meters and, in one B-17, a radio compass. In this state the B-17s crossed the Atlantic, took on some 500lb (227kg) bombs in Czechoslovakia and, using a small-scale map torn from an encyclopedia, bombed Cairo on their way to Israel.

As for the fighter, this was based on the formidable Messerschmitt Bf 109G, but because no DB 605 engines were available the Czechs put it into production with a dif-ferent engine and propeller that converted several previously poor characteristics into sheer murder. Combined with badly engineered and unreliable systems, notably the synchronizing gear for the fuselage guns, the Avia S 199 was undoubtedly more dangerous to its pilots than to its enemies. Few lasted more than a few weeks, but in that time the small number of combat sorties that were possible at least demonstrated that the infant Chel Ha'Avir was growing a few small teeth.

Light at the end of the tunnel came in the autumn of 1948 with the first Spitfires and P-51Ds. At

Above: Pictured here is Chel Ha'Avir hardware from the French Period; this is an SMB.2.

Below: Built in Israel, the Magister is being updated to continue in service to 1990.

the fighter base, Herzlia, the long poles strategically placed along the runway to enable rescuers to heave up the fuselage of inverted Avias so that the trapped pilot could open the canopy at last lay unused. The Chel Ha'Avir was becoming a real fighting force; but it was still immature and beset by difficulties at every turn.

The immaturity stemmed from the unique circumstances of its birth. Many pilots were *mahals*, Jewish and non-Jewish foreign volunteers. In the main these were men of long wartime experience, skilled in all aspects of front-line flying and often revelling in shooting down the enemy in a land of sunshine. The trouble was that, unlike other air forces, the Chel Ha'Avir consisted of combat pilots and ground crews and little else. There was no proper training organization, no engineering manuals, no training manuals, and the procedures were those adopted on the spot. The fighter squadron, No 101, would scramble its Spitfires first, then the P-51s and lastly the Avias which were likely to crash and block the runway. Camouflage and markings were whatever happened to be painted on the aircraft, and flying clothing was whatever the pilot happened to possess. Armament was whatever the fitters on the airfield had managed to bolt together, and squadron ground

transportation was a succession of cars 'borrowed' from the nearest town streets.

More seriously, the Knesset (Parliament) and the Defence Staff in Tel Aviv had no thought of building up an air force for propaganda purposes, and were pragmatic in the extreme. Money was tight and allocated according to a strict system of priorities that put much more emphasis on rifles for the kibbutz workers than on aeroplanes. The Chel Ha'Avir's political power was just about zero, and for the first five years it did not have any proper commander or command structure. Indeed, as the formidable *mahals* went back to their own countries from 1949 on, and the squadrons became popu-

Above: Bristol sleeve-valves will oscillate in the Noratlas transports until about 1986.

Below: The SA.321K Super Frelon helicopters have been upgraded with T58 engines.

lated by totally inexperienced young Israelis, the actual fighting ability probably declined despite the progressive introduction of better aircraft.

It was to a considerable extent the appointment of General Dan Tolkovski as C-in-C of the Chel Ha'Avir in 1953 that made the disorganized and extremely imperfect force pull itself together. By the start of the Suez War in October 1956 it had become an air force which in qualitative terms was second to none. Ever since, the public image has not been that of an indisciplined and wild rabble of mercenaries but of the most élite aviators imaginable.

It was during Tolkovski's vital leadership that France emerged as the source of Israel's airpower. Dassault provided the fighters, from the Ouragan through the Mystère IVA and Super Mystère B2 to the Mirage IIIC, by which time the Chel Ha'Avir was providing as much customer input as the Armée de l'Air itself. Sud-Aviation supplied the Vautour attack bombers, Nord the Noratlas transports, Potez Air Fouga the Magister jet trainer which was the first aircraft ever produced in Israel, and Sud-Aviation (later Aérospatiale) the turbine-powered Alouette II and the big Super Frelon helicopters. But in 1967 Général de Gaulle abruptly switched his nation's allegiance to the Arabs.

During the Six-Day War in June 1967 the Chel Ha'Avir achieved the swiftest and most complete victory over its several enemies ever gained by any air force. In the anti-air role these victories were spearheaded by the Mirage IIIC, which in Israeli hands was transformed almost overnight into the world's most publicised air-combat fighter and a global best-seller. During the preceding four years Israeli pilots and technicians, staff officers and civilian officials had worked closely with Dassault to produce a simplified Mirage with a heavier attack load for use in the clear skies of the Middle East. The result was the Mirage 5J, built to Israel's requirements, for which the Chel Ha'Avir purchased 50. By autumn 1967 these aircraft had been paid for in full, but de Gaulle refused to permit delivery. Knowing Israeli wiles, he ordered that when Chel Ha'Avir test pilots carried out test flights the tanks should be filled only sufficiently for a local flight in the Bordeaux area (every litre paid for). When the Chel Ha'Avir secured permission to carry out winter Mirage 5J conversion training in Corsica he had the aircraft dismantled just enough to make them unflyable and put into guarded storage. To rub salt into the wound, the French then charged Israel a fee for storing their Mirages, and later sold much larger numbers of almost identical Mirage 5s to Libya and Egypt.

Predictably this spurred the Israelis along a long and often

Above: The Kfir-C1, seen here rolling at low level with AAMs, marked new industrial capability.

Below: Security is a way of life in Israel; this S-65C-3 has its Service Number obliterated.

difficult road that led to their own manufacture of an Atar-powered Mirage, of a re-engined Mirage (J79 engine) and finally of a new fighter powered by the J79 engine and bearing only a superficial resemblance to the Mirage, the Kfir C2. In turn, this has given the Israelis confidence to tackle an even more challenging task: the creation of a combat aircraft for the 1990s from a clean sheet of paper.

It is an extraordinary fact that they have not — so far as one can tell — embarked on any kind of collaborative programme. We do not know what diplomatic interchanges took place in 1979–80 with Sweden, if any, but according to the published record Sweden is designing an advanced air-combat fighter and attack aircraft for the 1990s powered by the General Electric F404 (the engine of the twin-engined F-18) while Israel is designing an advanced air-combat fighter and attack aircraft for the 1990s powered by the Pratt & Whitney PW 1120 (which has not run as this is written, and has no other application). It is a fair guess that most of the clever systems of the Lavi, as the projected Israeli machine is called, will be American. US industry can thus be expected to crank in a lot of support and encouragement, but we are still a very long way from seeing a Lavi rolled out at Ben-Gurion airport. But 30 years ago that airport was a sandy waste littered with old wartime dumps which the Israelis picked over to find spare parts for small piston engines to keep their little aircraft flying. No other air force has come so far from literally nothing.

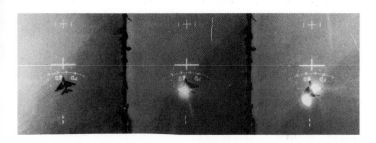

Above: Three exceptional combat camera frames taken in October 1973 by an Israeli F-4E pilot.

Below: Despite severe economic problems, the Chel Ha'Avir is in good shape: F-15 with afterburners.

Taylorcraft
Model C

Origin: Taylorcraft Aviation Corporation, Alliance, Ohio, USA; Taylorcraft Inc, Conway-Pittsburgh Airport, Pa, USA.
Type: Two-seat light trainer and transport.
Engine: (Most) one 55hp Lycoming O-145-A2 or 65hp O-145-B2; (some) 65hp Continental A-65 or O-170-3; all four-cylinder opposed piston engines.
Dimensions: Span 36ft 0in (10·97m); length (typical) 22ft 0in (6·71m); height 6ft 6in to 6ft 8in (max 2·03m); wing area 183·5sq ft (17·05m²).
Weights (typical): Empty 700lb (318kg); loaded (max) 1,200lb (544kg).
Performance: Maximum speed (typical) 105mph (169km/h); cruising speed 90mph (145km/h); initial climb 450–550ft/min (2·3–2·8m/s); range 250–350 miles (402–563km).
History: First flight (Model A) late 1936, (D) 1941, (L-2, then designated YO-57) 1941.

C. G. Taylor designed the original Cub high-wing monoplane in 1930, production starting the following year. In 1936 Mr Taylor started Taylor Aviation, the original company becoming Piper Aircraft Corporation. Three Model C side-by-side trainers were bought in 1938–39 by the Palestine Flying Service, and used for flight training from Lod airport. At the outbreak of World War 2, the three aircraft were sold to the Aviron company. Two of them entered service with Sherut Avir in November 1947; this became Chel Ha'Avir in May 1948. They were used for any covert missions that they could tackle.

Right: The three pre-war Taylorcraft Model C trainers with pilots of Palestine Flying Service; date probably 1939.

RWD
RWD.8, 13 and 15

Origin: Doswiadczalne Warsztaty Lotnicze, Lodz, Poland.
Type: (8) two-seat tandem trainer, (13) three-seat cabin tourer, (15) five-seat transport.
Engine: (8) one 110hp Walter Junior; (13, 15) one 125hp Walter-built DH Gipsy Major; all four-cylinder inverted inline.
Dimensions: Span (8) 36ft 1in (11·0m), (13) 38ft 0$\frac{2}{3}$in (11·6m); length (8) 26ft 3in (8·0m), (13) 25ft 9in (7·85m); height (8) 7ft 6in (2·29m), (13) 6ft 6$\frac{3}{4}$in (2·0m); wing area (8) 215sq ft (20·0m²), (13) 172sq ft (16m²).
Weights: Empty (8) 1,056lb (479kg), (13) 1,764lb (800kg); maximum loaded (8) 1,664lb (755kg), (13) 2,046lb (928kg).
Performance: Maximum speed (8) 110mph (177km/h), (13) 132mph (212km/h); ceiling (8) 16,404ft (5km), (13) 13,770ft (4197m); range (8) 272 miles (438km), (13) 563 miles (906km).
History: First flight (8) 1932, (13) July 1935, (15) 1938.

The design team of Rogalski, Wigura and Drzwiecki produced a major series of Polish lightplanes throughout the 1930s, almost all with fuselages of welded steel tube and wings of wood, with fabric covering. In 1946 the Palestine Civilian Flying Club relied very heavily on its pre-war RWDs: RWD.8s VQ-PAG and PAK; RWD. 13s VQ-PAL and PAM; and the RWD.15 VQ-PAE. The 8s could fly virtually anywhere, and had the advantage of folding wings for concealment, but they were almost falling apart. The RAF assisted with Tiger spares and provided air traffic control at

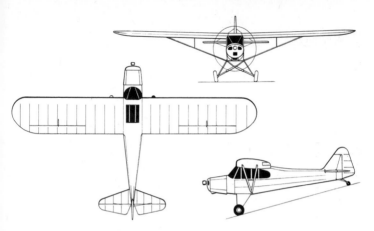

Above: Three-view of Taylorcraft Model C.

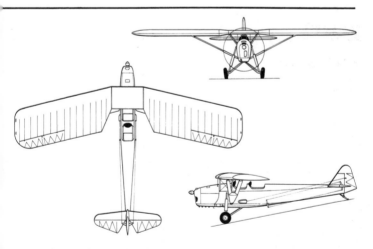

Above: The RWD.8s were silver with blue cowls and wing struts.

Ramleh for what it believed to be "taxi and charter work". The two 13s were pressed into service with Sherut Avir when it was formed in November 1947. One of them was destroyed on the ground in an Egyptian air attack on 15 May 1948, but the second continued serving with Chel Ha'Avir until the end of the War of Independence. The RWD.15 was destroyed at Lod airport on 13 April 1948; however, neither it nor the two 8s served with Sherut Avir or Chel Ha'Avir.

Auster

Auster AOP.5 and J/1 Autocrat

Origin: (AOP) Taylorcraft Aeroplanes (England), Britannia Works, Thurmaston, Leicester; (J/1) Auster Aircraft Ltd, Rearsby Aerodrome, Leicester.
Type: (AOP) 2/3-seater, (J/1) 3/4-seat cabin lightplane.
Engine: (AOP) one 130hp Lycoming O-290-3/1 four-cylinder opposed; (J/1) one 100hp Blackburn Cirrus Minor 2 inverted four-cylinder inline.
Dimensions: Span 36ft 0in (10·97m); length (AOP) 22ft 5in (6·83m), (J/1) 23ft 5in (7·14m); height (both) 8ft 0in (2·44m); wing area (AOP) 167sq ft (15·5m²), (J/1) 185sq ft (17·19m²).
Weights: Empty (AOP) 1,160lb (526kg), (J/1) 1,052lb (477kg); maximum loaded (AOP) 1.990lb (903kg), (J/1) 1,850lb (839kg).
Performance: Maximum speed (AOP) 130mph (209km/h), (J/1) 118mph (190km/h); cruise (both) 105mph (169km/h); ceiling 15,000ft (4572m); range (AOP) 250 miles (402km), (J/1) 320 miles (515km).
History: First flight (AOP) 1943, (J/1) 1945.

Standard light AOP (air observation post) with the British Army during World War 2, the various marks of Auster saw service in all theatres, including Palestine. Their tough welded-steel structure was unaffected by heat, rain or sandstorms, and the AOP.5, with US engine and blind-flying instruments, was a most serviceable aircraft that could land almost anywhere. It was used as the basis for the first post-war civil version, the J/1 Autocrat, which

DH Dragon Rapide

DH.89A Dragon Rapide

Origin: The de Havilland Aircraft Co, Hatfield, England; wartime production by other companies.
Type: Light transport, used as bomber.
Engines: Two 200hp DH Gipsy Six Series I inverted six-inline.
Dimensions: Span 48ft 0in (14·63m); length 34ft 6in (10·52m); height 10ft 3in (3·12m); wing area 336sq ft (31·2m²).
Weights: Empty about 3,200lb (1452kg); maximum loaded 5,500lb (2495kg).
Performance: Maximum speed (new) 157mph (253km/h); cruising speed 124mph (200km/h); ceiling 16,000ft (4·9km); range 520 miles (837km).
Armament: Locally equipped with ex-RAF bomb racks for four bombs of 250lb (113·4kg) size or various smaller weapons.
History: First flight (prototype) April 1934; Israeli aircraft manufactured 1937.

Below: Three-view of DH.89A.

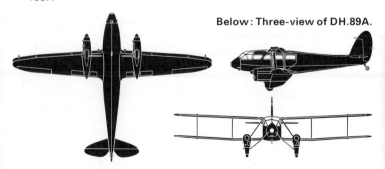

however went into production with a British engine of lower power but burning only 4 Imp gal per hour in cruising flight. Several J/1 Autocrats were bought by customers in Palestine, one of the first being VQ-PAS (ex G-AHHV) which reached Ramleh in late 1946. The following year the British sold a whole scrap-dump of wartime Austers to Aviron, the Palestinian aircraft-import firm, for £14,000. As soon as the deal was concluded the British tried to cancel, but by then the hardware was being rebuilt into flying Austers. By late 1947 there were at least 15 Mk 5s and five J/1s. Numerically they were the most important in the infant state of Israel, and they flew hundreds of missions in May 1948, not only for supply and reconnaissance but also on 'bombing' sorties with grenades and home-made bombs, the largest being a 125lb (56·7kg) drum pushed by hand from the cabin.

Below: A local variant unknown elsewhere was this Auster AOP.5 re-engined with the Gipsy Major I inline engine.

One Dragon Rapide light transport (VQ-PAC) operated air services with Palestine Airways during the British mandate in Palestine in 1939. It continued flying during the war for the RAF. A second (VQ-PAR) was acquired in 1947 by the Aviron company for post-war civil transport services. Doped silver (possibly the original colour scheme) it had six passenger seats in 1947. Curiously it had no windmill-driven generator, though it had a battery-fed electrical system for night-flying. This single Rapide entered service with Sherut Avir in November 1947. (Three more Rapides were acquired in England in May 1948 and flown to Israel.) When Israel was born, this aged and low-powered wood/fabric biplane was its largest and most important single aircraft, and it was speedily converted into a bomber. It is known that it once carried four 250lb (113·4kg) British-type bombs, though the usual load was probably less and weapons of 40lb (18.1kg) and 200lb (90·7kg) size are also said to have been dropped. No bombsight was fitted. The number of combat missions flown was not fewer than eight and was probably much greater, all by day and often at very low level over invading armies. The high spot was unquestionably the attack on the Egyptian invasion fleet heading for Tel Aviv on 4 June 1948. This aircraft was still flying in early 1949, an incredible achievement in the circumstances.

Below: Preserved Rapide with winged-6 emblem on tail.

Beechcraft Bonanza
Model 35

Origin: Beech Aircraft Corporation, Wichita, Kansas, USA.
Type: Four-seat cabin monoplane.
Engine: One 185hp Continental E-185-1 or -3, six-cylinder opposed.
Dimensions: Span 32ft 10in (10·0m); length 25ft 2in (7·67m); height 6ft 6½in (2·0m); wing area 177·6sq ft (16·50m²).
Weights: Empty 1,541lb (699kg); maximum loaded 2,650lb (1202kg).
Performance: Maximum speed 184mph (296km/h); cruising speed 170mph (274km/h); ceiling 17,500ft (5334m); range (as built) 750 miles (1207km).
Armament: Fitted with racks under wing roots for various bomb loads including two of 200lb (90·7kg) size; some were fitted for firing small arms from within the cabin (apparently through hinged panels in the windows).
History: First flight 22 December 1945.

In the years immediately following World War 2 the V-tailed Bonanza was the most sought-after lightplane in the world (it still looks modern today, and remains in production). Three of the first to be seen in southern Africa were all purchased by Boris Senior, who had flown with the wartime SAAF and subsequently devoted himself to the Israeli cause. The first two left Johannesburg about June 1947 and headed north. One was flown by the author on its stop-over in Southern Rhodesia on a so-called 'pleasure trip

---

Noorduyn Norseman
C-64A Norseman

Origin: Noorduyn Aviation Ltd, Montreal.
Type: Utility transport.
Engine: One 600hp Pratt & Whitney R-1340-AN1 Wasp nine-cylinder radial.
Dimensions: Span 51ft 8in (15·8m); length 31ft 9in (9·68m); height 10ft 1in (3·08m); wing area 325sq ft (30·19m²).
Weights: Empty about 4,700lb (2132kg); maximum loaded 7,400lb (3357kg).
Performance: Maximum speed 155mph (249km/h); cruising speed 141mph (227km/h); ceiling 17,000ft (5182m); range 442 miles (711km).
Armament: None, but first example equipped to drop bombs.
History: First flight late 1935, (C-64) 1942.

Below: The arrival in spring 1948 of 17 Norsemen more than doubled the horsepower of the infant Chel Ha'Avir!

Above: The bomb racks are clearly seen under the first Bonanza in the Negev in May 1948. Later two other Bonanzas reached Israel.

to Europe'; he never guessed Senior and ferry-pilot Katz were going to help form the Israeli air force, though this had been suspected in Johannesburg. Neither of the first two completed the long journey, but the third, flown by Senior, reached Luxor in southern Egypt, refuelled and landed next not at the published destination of Beirut but in the Negev. The sleek aircraft was soon converted into as warlike a machine as possible, and as the flagship of the Tel Aviv squadron flew many combat missions including the amazing repulsion of the Egyptian invasion fleet on 4 June 1948, and a bombing attack on Amman, Jordan.

Famed as the most successful of pre-war Canadian 'bush' transports, largely because of its Wasp engine, the Norseman had fabric covering over wooden wings and a steel-tube fuselage and was widely used on wheels, skis and floats. In 1940 it became a radio/nav trainer with the RCAF, and in 1942–45 the C-64 utility version was adopted as a standard vehicle with the USAAF. Licence production by Aeronca was cancelled before first delivery, and the Canadian company delivered 746 plus a further three to the US Navy. In early 1948 agents (posing as representatives of a Belgian airline) managed to buy 20 ex-USAF machines, of which 17 reached Israel. One was deliberately sabotaged by Arab agents, exploding as it left Rome Urbe on 20 May 1948, killing Canada's famed wartime ace G. F. 'Screwball' Buerling. Two more landed by mistake at Gaza in Egyptian territory. The 17 Norsemen were quickly fitted with previously prepared racks for four bombs (believed of 250lb [113·4kg] size). They were the most powerful aircraft in the embryo Sherut Avir, and were invaluable in providing virtually all the front-line airlift during the first weeks of Israel's existence. They proved highly resistant to flak and easy to repair, but few survived more than 18 months.

Below: Standard C-64A Norseman landplane as used by Israel.

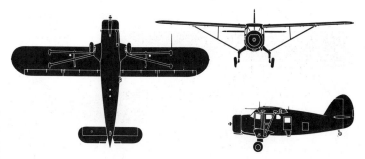

DH Tiger Moth

DH.82C

Origin: de Havilland Aircraft of Canada Ltd, Downsview, Toronto.
Type: Tandem-seat biplane.
Engine: One 130hp DH Gipsy Major four-cylinder inverted inline.
Dimensions: Span 29ft 4in (8·94m); length 23ft 11in (7·29m); height 8ft 9½in (2·68m); wing area 239sq ft (22·2m²).
Weights: Empty 1,121lb (508·5kg); loaded 1,825lb (828kg).
Performance: Maximum speed 109mph (175km/h); cruising speed 89mph (143km/h); ceiling 17,900ft (5·5km); range 290 miles (467km).
Armament: None
History: First flight October 1931.

In late 1946 the Civilian Flying Club received permission from the British authorities to import two ex-RCAF Tiger Moths. These arrived in early March 1947, registered CF-CJA and -CTB. They were standard dual trainers with sliding cockpit hoods and Gipsy engines (a few DH.82C aircraft had the Menasco Pirate C4). They were painted, one in yellow and the other black, and registered VQ-PAU and -PAV. In about June 1947 they were joined by a British-built Tiger which became VQ-PAN, but only the Canadian aircraft entered Sherut Avir service. They flew front-line

Fairchild F-24

F-24R (UC-61F)

Origin: Fairchild Engine & Airplane Corporation, Hagerstown, Maryland.
Type: Utility four-seater.
Engine: One 165hp Ranger 6-410-B1 six-cylinder inverted inline.
Dimensions: Span 36ft 4in (11·07m); length 23ft 10½ (7·28m); height 7ft 7½in (2·3m); wing area 193·3sq ft (17·96m²).
Weights: Empty 1,525lb (692kg); maximum loaded 2,550lb (1157kg).
Performance: Maximum speed 125mph (201km/h); cruising speed 112mph (180km/h); ceiling 13,500ft (4·1km); range 550 miles (885km).
Armament: Briefly equipped to drop bombs (see text).
History: First flight (Model 24) 1932, (-24R) 1938.

Below: Three-view of Fairchild F-24R without local modifications.

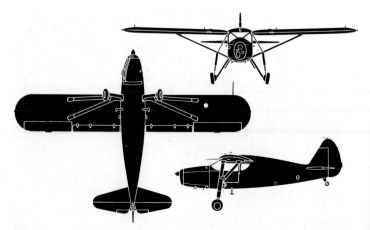

Above: Tiger Moth II (early series) with fuselage bomb rack.

supply, reconnaissance and even attack missions (using grenades from the cockpit and, briefly, light bombs released by makeshift racks under the fuselage). Both were destroyed in action in May 1948.

The pre-war F-24R was one of the versions of one of the best-selling four-seat high-wing cabin aircraft in the world in the late 1940s, large numbers of which were used during the war by the US forces as the UC-61 Forwarder (Navy, GK-1) and by the RAF and Commonwealth as the Argus. The R was one of the models with Fairchild's own inline Ranger engine. Accommodation was provided on four padded seats, though in Israeli service a single bucket seat was substituted for a pilot with seat-type parachute. A single F-24R was being used by an Egyptian hashish smuggler, and on one of its trips to Palestine in March 1948 it was captured by the Haganah (Zionist defence force) and pressed into service as an Israeli civil machine. In May 1948 it was equipped to carry bombs; it is not known whether these were hung under the fuselage or wings. At least one of the rear windows was removed to enable a machine gun to be fired from the cabin. The Fairchild was shot down by the invading Egyptian ships heading for Tel Aviv on 4 June 1948.

Below: Using a hand-held plate camera, with the door removed, was the 1948 recon system! Badge is the 3rd Palmach "The Galil".

Piper Cub

J3C, PA-11 Cub Special and PA-18 Super Cub

L-4H, L-4J and PA-18 Super Cub

Origin: Piper Aircraft Corporation, Lock Haven, Pennsylvania.
Type: Observation and utility two-seater.
Engine: (J3) one 65hp Continental O-170-3, (PA-18) one 125hp or 150hp Lycoming O-290D; all four-cylinder opposed.
Dimensions: Span 32ft 2½in (10·73m); length (J3) 22ft 0in (6·7m), (PA) 22ft 4½in (6·82m); height 6ft 8in (2·03m); wing area 178·5sq ft (16·58m²).
Weights: Empty (J3) about 730lb (331kg), (PA) 805lb (365kg); maximum loaded (J3) 1,220lb (553kg), (PA) 1,500lb (680kg).
Performance: Maximum speed (J3) 87mph (140km/h), (PA) 110mph (177km/h); cruising speed (J3) 75mph (121km/h), (PA) 100mph (161km/h); ceiling (J3) 9,500ft (2·9km), (PA) 16,400ft (5km); range (J3) 190 miles (306km), (PA) 770 miles (1239km).
Armament: Some fitted to drop bombs (see text).
History: First flight (Taylor Cub) 1931, (Piper) 1937.

The first three Piper Cubs entered Chel Ha'Avir service in late 1948 or early 1949. Able to use any flat strip, these were ideal observation and liaison machines, but unable to carry much. A real windfall was the ap-

Republic Seabee

RC-3

Origin: Republic Aviation Corporation, Farmingdale, NY.
Type: Four-seat utility amphibian.
Engine: One 215hp Franklin 6A8-215-B7F six-cylinder opposed.
Dimensions: Span 37ft 8in (11·48m); length 27ft 11in (8·51m); height 10ft 1in (3·07m); wing area 196sq ft (18·21m²).
Weights: Empty 1.963lb (890kg); loaded 3,000lb (1361kg).
Performance: Maximum speed 120mph (193km/h); cruising speed 98 mph (158km/h); ceiling 11,700ft (3566m); range (75gal) 560 miles (900km).
History: First flight (RC-1) November 1944, (RC-3) December 1945.

Below: Three-view of RC-3 Seabee with landing gear raised.

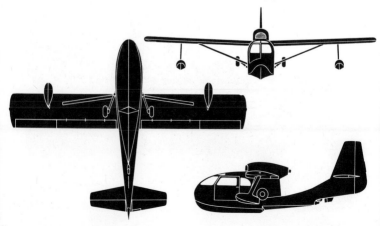

Above: The PA-18-150 Super Cub is used for pupil-pilot grading.

parently legitimate purchase of 20 post-war Super Cubs from the United States in May 1948, during the first war of independence. These were PA-18s with the relatively powerful cowled Lycoming engine (same engine as in the Auster 5) and the military-type glazing extended back over the rear fuselage. For ten years they were the chief Chel Ha'Avir lightplanes, in their early days making countless front-line bombing missions with 44lb (20kg) bombs. At first the pilots carried these on their laps but by July 1948 they were released from under-fuselage racks. About 100 PA-18-150 Super Cubs were purchased from Piper in the period 1956–1968. This aircraft currently serves for primary training at the Chel Ha'Avir flying school.

It was a bold step for Republic, famed builder of the P-47 fighter, to launch a radically advanced four-seat amphibian for the private market. Whereas Republic's predecessor, Seversky, had made costly high-speed amphibians, the Seabee was aimed at cheap flying from any airstrip or smooth water. All-metal stressed-skin structure was simplified for easy mass-production, and the comfortable cabin with large side doors was well ahead of the engine and gave a perfect all-round view (except to directly astern, and interception by Spitfires was not exactly a design consideration). Sadly, the Seabee was a poor performer, sluggish and unresponsive. The specimen imported by M. Tsopek (NC-6731K), a lawyer in Palestine in 1947, had a charmed life and lasted longer than most of its brethren in more congenial places. Impressed into the Sherut Avir, it was flown intensively, suffered several forced landings and did an amazing amount of work; but it was heartily disliked. It was destroyed on the ground on 15 May 1948.

Below: Offical records give the Chel Ha'Avir number of the Seabee as 60, while the aircraft itself was numbered 61!

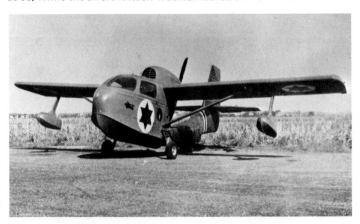

Douglas C-47

Sub-types not known

Origin: Douglas Aircraft Company, Santa Monica, California; made only at Tulsa and Long Beach.
Type: Transport.
Engines: Two 1,200hp Pratt & Whitney R-1830-92 Twin Wasp 14-cylinder radials.
Dimensions: Span 95ft 0in (28·96m); length 64ft 5½in (19·65m); height 16ft 11¼in (5·16m); wing area 987sq ft (91·69m²).
Weights: Empty about 16,970lb (7698kg); loaded 26,000lb (11,794kg); normal maximum cargo load 6,000lb (2722kg).
Performance: Maximum speed 229mph (369km/h); cruising speed 180mph (290km/h); service ceiling 23,200ft (7km); range 1,500 miles (2414km).
Armament: None, but bombs fitted to at least one aircraft (see text).
History: First flight (DST) 17 December 1935, (C-47) December 1941, delivered 1 February 1942.

By far the most famous and widely used transport in history, the DC-3 was soon developed via the C-41 of 1938 into the C-47 of which almost 11,000 (including variants) were built during 1942–45. The first three Dakotas were acquired by Israel from Universal Airways of South Africa at the end of 1947. They subsequently entered service with the Chel Ha'Avir in the summer of 1948, having been refurbished. As they were far more powerful than any other aircraft in Israeli hands they were an obvious choice for conversion into bombers. It is not known how many were thus equipped, but the first, a Long Beach-built C-47 which became Sherut Avir No 18, was certainly rigged to carry more than two tons (this meant short tons of 2,000lb) of bombs of 200 to 250lb (90·7 to 113·4kg) size. These were

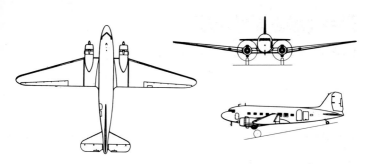

Above: Three-view of typical C-47 (all generally similar).

carried in a row on the cargo floor and rolled out by hand through the door when roughly over the target, the rolling being controlled by rods inserted into holes in the floor. Various accounts give the impression that at least one C-47 was later equipped with a bombsight and conventional external racks, but this has proved impossible to confirm. What is beyond dispute is that the various C-47, C-53 and Dakota transports acquired by the Chel Ha'Avir were by far the best and most capable trucking aircraft available until the Noratlas arrived in 1956. Altogether, in 1948–60 at least 24 were put into service, some purchased from US stocks and five freely loaned by a wealthy Dutchman and a South African civil company (not SAA). Most were still active in the 1970s, and even in the early 1980s a nominal total of 18 were on charge though some are not active. Most of these were purchased after 1960, and though serial numbers have changed it appears that none of the 1948 'bombers' is left.

Below: Still important in the Chel Ha'Avir the C-47 series has numerous local modifications including modified tailwheel legs.

Curtiss Commando

C-46A, C-46D

Origin: Curtiss-Wright Corporation, NY; built at Buffalo and Louisville.
Type: Cargo transport.
Engines: Two 2,000hp Pratt & Whitney R-2800-51 Double Wasp 18-cylinder two-row radials.
Dimensions: Span 108ft 1in (32·94m); length 76ft 4in (23·26m); height (tail down) 21ft 9in (6·63m); wing area 1,360sq ft (126·35m²).
Weights: Empty 32,400lb (14,967kg); maximum loaded 56,000lb (25,402kg).
Performance: Maximum speed (max wt) 234mph (377km/h); cruising speed 183mph (295km/h); service ceiling 24,500ft (7·47km); range 1,200 miles (1931km).
History: First flight (CW-20) March 1940, (C-46) May 1942.

Potentially the most advanced and most capable twin-engined transport ever built by 1940, the CW-20 was intended as a luxurious 36-passenger airliner. Instead it was rapidly developed to far heavier weights as a tough military freighter, though with provision for 50 tip-up troop seats or 33 stretchers (litters) plus four medical attendants as alternatives to 10,000lb (4536kg) of cargo loaded through large side doors on to a a sloping floor 118in (3m) wide with multiple tiedown rings and special tracks for loading heavy cargo such as engines. Further cargo could be loaded under the floor and propellers could be attached under the fuselage. In World War 2 its allegedly good high-altitude performance saw it operated in large numbers over 'The Hump' and other tough routes, but in fact engine-out performance was non-existent even at the reduced gross weight of 45,000lb (20,412kg). The first for the Sherut Avir flew from Teterboro, NJ, on 6 March 1948. It was followed by nine others, and eventually — after an

Douglas DC-4 Skymaster

C-54D

Origin: Douglas Aircraft Company, Santa Monica, California; built at Chicago.
Type: Long-range transport.
Engines: Four 1,350hp Pratt & Whitney R-2000-11 Twin Wasp 14-cylinder two-row radials.
Dimensions: Span 117ft 6in (35·81m); length 93ft 11in (28·63m); height 27ft 6¼in (8·39m); wing area 1,460sq ft (135·6m²).
Weights: Empty about 38,000lb (17,240kg); maximum loaded 73,000lb (33,113kg).
Performance: Maximum speed 265mph (426km/h); cruising speed (typical) 210mph (338km/h); service ceiling 22,500ft (6858m); range with maximum payload of 16,500lb (7484kg), 1,500 miles (2414km); max range with 5,400lb (2·45t) cargo at 190mph (306km/h), 3,900 miles (6276km).
History: First flight (DC-4E) June 1938, (C-54) 26 March 1942.

In late 1947, when serious searching for future Israeli military aircraft began, the C-54 was the most capable transport generally available. The first to serve Israel was chartered from American Overseas Airlines (subsidiary of American Airlines) in March 1948, ferrying war material from Czechoslovakia (including the first two S 199s). On the day war began, 15 May 1948, the newly created Sherut Avir purchased two war-surplus C-54s released

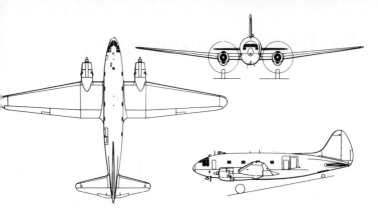

Above: Three-view of C-46A (all models generally similar).

incredible series of adventures — eight arrived in Israel. Despite incessant engine failures and other problems they shuttled around the clock, mainly bringing arms and dismantled S 199 fighters from Czechoslovakia but also acting as lead ships for the Spitfires and on at least one occasion serving as bombers (over El Arish).

Below: A Chel Ha'Avir C-46 on a paratroop training mission.

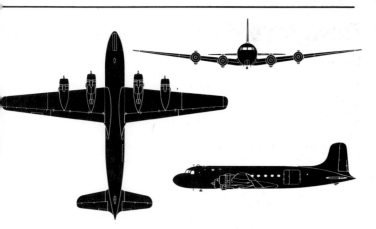

Above: Three-view of C-54D as operated by the Chel Ha'Avir.

ostensibly for airline use. These were not, as sometimes reported, postwar DC-4s; the latter had quite different loading arrangements, with a small cargo door forward on the right and a passenger door on the left. Able to carry an overload of 32,000lb (14·5t) cargo, or up to 50 troops, the two C-54Ds, called DC-4s, operated in civil markings when on overseas trips, such as bringing supplies from Czechoslovakia (when they acted as lead ships for Spitfires).

Lockheed Constellation
Model 049 (ex C-69)

Origin: Lockheed Aircraft Corporation, Burbank, California.
Type: Long-range transport.
Engines: Four 2,200hp Wright R-3350-35 Duplex Cyclone 18-cylinder two-row radials.
Dimensions: Span 123ft 0in (37·49m); length 95ft 1¼in (28·99m); height 23ft 8in (7·21m); wing area 1,650sq ft (153·29m²).
Weights: Empty 50,500lb (22,907kg); loaded 86,250lb (39,123kg).
Performance: Maximum speed 330mph (531km/h); cruising speed (typical) 259mph (417km/h); service ceiling 24,600ft (7·5km); range with 20,000lb (9t) payload, 2,280 miles (3670km).
History: First flight 9 January 1943.

Planned as a pressurized civil passenger airliner, the Constellation was the world's fastest, most powerful and most complex transport during World War 2. The original batch of 22 requisitioned or ordered by the Army Air Force were declared surplus in 1947 and for $45,000 Al Schwimmer managed by clandestine methods to purchase three for a non-existent Panamanian airline. They spent the winter 1947—48 being completely overhauled by Schwimmer Aviation at Burbank, but the FBI caught up with two and impounded them. The third, painted in the markings of Lineas Aereas de Panama, had already left for the Canal Zone in company with the last five

Avro Anson
652M Anson I

652M Anson I
Origin: A. V. Roe & Co, Chadderton, Manchester.
Type: Trainer and utility transport.
Engines: Two 320hp Armstrong Siddeley Cheetah IX seven-cylinder radials.
Dimensions: Span 56ft 6in (17·22m); length 42ft 3in (12·88m); height 13ft 1in (3·99m); wing area 463sq ft (43·0m²).
Weights: Empty about 5,375lb (2438kg); loaded 8,000lb (3629kg).
Performance: Maximum speed 188mph (303km/h); cruising speed 150mph (241km/h); service ceiling 19,200ft (5·85km); range 700 miles (1126km).
Armament: Equipped to carry bombs (as built, internal wing bays for two 100lb [45·4kg] and eight 20lb [9·1kg] bombs plus two 250lb [113kg] external).
History: First flight 24 March 1935.

The Sherut Avir managed to acquire four Anson Is in Britain in early 1948, but all were impounded by the Greek government on the island of Rhodes on their way to Israel and were allowed to proceed only after the War of Independence had ended in 1949. They were unusual in having plain instead of helmeted cowlings, and had served in the RAF. Painted yellow, they served as multi-engine pilot and navigator trainers. At least one had a standard course-setting bombsight, and two (probably all) were fitted with D/F loop aerials in acorn fairings above the fuselage. The common report that an Anson operated as a bomber during the 1948 war is untrue; the Israelis were unable to bring them the last 480 miles (772km). Four more Mk Is arrived later: G-ALVN and VO (ex-LT452 and LV320) in April 1950, G-ALXE (pre-war N9785) a month later, and G-ALFP (ex-NK971) in October 1952.

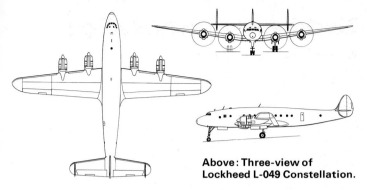

**Above: Three-view of
Lockheed L-049 Constellation.**

C-46s. The whole fleet then managed to leave Panama on 8 May 1948 and cross the Atlantic. The L-049, still with Panamanian registration RX-121, reached Czechoslovakia and loaded with war cargo. This aircraft made seven cargo flights during the initial war phase, and was later joined by its two sisters which were released from US detention when it appeared that they were genuinely destined for use by El Al. In fact, these three aircraft continued to bring urgent supplies to the Negev base at least as often as they flew passengers to Lydda. After El Al was formed in April 1949, they were transferred to commercial service. Later, in October 1953, El Al bought 049E N74192, previously G-AHEN of BOAC; she became 4X-AKD and served seven years.

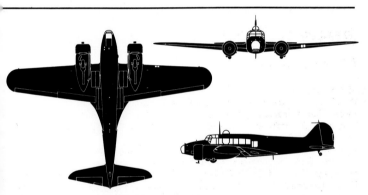

Above: Three-view of Anson with plain cowlings (but glazed nose).

Below: One of the Anson Is rebuilt with separate cabin windows, a passenger door on the right side and two astro domes.

Boeing B-17

B-17G

Origin: Boeing Airplane Company, Seattle, Washington (also made by Douglas at Tulsa and Vega at Burbank).
Type: Bomber.
Engines: Four 1,200hp Wright R-1820-97 Cyclone nine-cylinder radials.
Dimensions: Span 103ft 9in (31·6m); length 74ft 9in (22·8m); height 19ft 1in (5·8m); wing area 1,420sq ft (131·92m²).
Weights (as built): Empty 35,800lb (16,238kg); maximum loaded 65,600lb (29,756kg).
Performance: When new, maximum speed 287mph (462km/h); cruising speed 182mph (293km/h); service ceiling 35,000ft (10,670m); range with 6,000lb (2722kg) bombload, 2,000 miles (3219km).
Armament: As originally operated by Chel Ha'Avir, usual bombload twelve 500lb (227kg); no guns. By October 1948 a scheme involving eight 0·5in (12·7mm) Brownings had been studied but only waist guns had been fitted.
History: First flight (Model 299) 28 July 1935, (production B-17B) June 1939.

Acquisition of four B-17 Fortresses was by far the biggest single advance in the entire embryonic period of Israeli airpower. The story is typically shot through with intrigue. Masterminded by Yehuda Arazi, the purchase was actually completed by Al Schwimmer via an undercover office in New York, literally hours ahead of the FBI, and in early June 1948 the aircraft were readied for a series of long flights fraught with danger. Only three could be made safe, and none was fully certificated. Unlike hundreds of B-17s in the 'Boneyard' at Davis-Monthan AFB, these three B-17Gs were flying disasters. They had been roughly stripped of every item of military gear and of most of their radio and navigation equipment. Crude sheets of aluminium and plywood not quite filled gaps where turrets had been, the bomb doors

Above: After 1949 the Chel Ha'Avir B-17s operated in the maritime role with ASH nose radar.

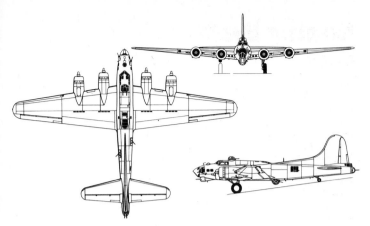

Above: Three-view of B-17G as originally built.

were sealed by riveted strips and many items had been vandalised. Flying in loose formation with US markings they reached Puerto Rico and then took off ostensibly for Recife, Brazil, but in fact flew non-stop to Lajes, Azores. When they got there they heard the US Ambassador to Portugal was about to arrive to arrest the aircraft, so they took off in dense fog and eventually reached Zatec, Czechoslovakia. Here they took on Chel Ha'Avir identity, and were fitted with various lash-up fits to enable them to drop bombs. On 15 July they left Zatec with full tanks and four 500lb (227kg) bombs apiece, as well as a fair load of urgent stores. They were shot at off the Albanian coast, and then by various routes reached Cairo after nightfall and bombed the Egyptian capital before going to Israel. Subsequently they formed the 69th Sqn, Ha-Patishim (The Hammers), based usually at Ramat David. They flew missions to more than 40 targets, and were almost unique among Israeli warplanes in remaining airworthy for many years. They were retired shortly after the 1956 Suez war when they bombed Gaza.

Above: One of the early B-17s, probably No 1601, seen from its partner while operating in the sea patrol role in the early 1950s. Its bomb racks are empty.

Left: No 1602 in 1948 markings. By 1950 it had been rebuilt with dorsal and ball turrets fitted and a chin bulge for photography. By this time it was in natural metal finish.

31

North American T-6

AT-6 (postwar T-6) Texan/Harvard, most AT-6D and AT-16

Origin: North American Aviation, Inglewood, California; made by other plants and licensees.
Type: Pilot trainer and light attack.
Engine: One 550hp Pratt & Whitney R-1340-49 or -AN1 Wasp nine-cylinder radial.
Dimensions: Span 42ft 0¼in (12·8m); length 29ft 6in (8·99m); height 11ft 8½in (3·56m); wing area 254sq ft (23·6m²).
Weights: Empty about 4,000lb (1814kg); loaded 5,275lb (2393kg).
Performance: Maximum speed 210mph (338km/h); cruising speed 145mph (233km/h); service ceiling 24,000ft (7·3km); range 630 miles (1014km).
Armament: Various, including Browning machine gun(s) firing ahead and (rare in Israel) third similar weapon aimed from rear cockpit; light series wing bomb racks locally modified to carry non-standard weapons with possible total weight of 500lb (227kg).
History: First flight (NA-26) 1937, (AT-6D) 1942.

Though designed as a trainer, and produced in vast numbers (just over 20,000) in many variants in 1936–52, the prolific T-6 family has also occasionally found employment as a front-line combat aircraft, even into the 1970s. Thanks to its almost unbreakable all-metal structure, it proved to be one of the few early types pressed into use by the infant Chel Ha'Avir to last more than a few weeks. Indeed large numbers served as the standard advanced trainer throughout the 1950s.

The first ten were acquired by typically roundabout means during the initial weeks of the Jewish state, but no way could be found to bring them to Israel after the lifting of the embargo, and none entered Chel Ha'Avir service until 2 November 1948. This initial batch were immediately pressed into use as front-line close-support aircraft, with military camouflage (with various schemes of yellow bands to distinguish them from almost identical Syrian aircraft). Several accounts claim that they carried two 0·50in (12·7mm) guns firing ahead, one on the left wing and the other above the engine; this was a non-standard armament unknown to the original design authority and was clearly designed locally (though at that time there was no Israeli aircraft organization with any approved certification). Wing racks were fitted for eight 110lb (50kg) bombs. Based at Eqron with 35 Flight, the aircraft were known as Harvards and flew their first dive-bombing mission over Falluja in December. Their attacks at about 70° proved generally

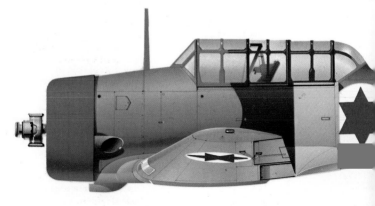

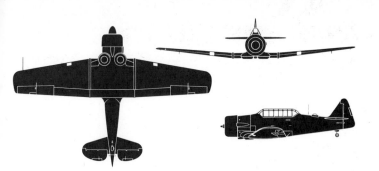

Above: Three-view of T-6D (with D/F aerial in rear fuselage).

more accurate than the crude level bombing by converted transports, and they were continually in action.

In early 1949 a further 25 AT-6Ds were purchased in France. Additional T-6s which arrived in Israel in 1953 brought the total to 90. These equipped the first properly organized advanced pilot training unit in Israel, and at first merely had provision for armament. Livery was all-yellow, with a black anti-dazzle panel, and the rear cockpit was equipped for an instructor rather than an observer. Armament options included a forward-firing 0·303in (7·7mm) Browning in the right-wing root, eight 110lb (50kg) bombs or tubes for 16 Hotchkiss-Brandt 3·15in (80mm) rockets. Fully armed, they saw action just once, during the Suez war of October-November 1956. They flew 24 bomb and rocket sorties, losing two aircraft shot down.

Above: This aircraft, probably an AT-6D, has light series wing bomb racks and appears also to have a gun in the inboard right wing. Stripe colour unknown.

Left: Whereas the photograph above dates from about 1949 this aircraft is shown in markings of the mid-1950s, when the large fleet (called Harvards) were all trainers.

Avia S 199

S 199 Mezek

Origin: Czech national industry at Avia works, Cakovice, and Letov works, Letnany.
Type: Single-seat fighter.
Engine: One 1,350hp Junkers Jumo 211F inverted-vee-12.
Dimensions: Span 32ft 6½in (9·92m); length 29ft 10¼in (9·10m); height 8ft 6in (2·59m); wing area 173·3sq ft (16·1m²).
Weights: Empty 5,732lb (2600kg); loaded 7,716lb (3500kg).
Performance: Maximum speed 367mph (590km/h); cruising speed 249mph (400km/h); service ceiling 31,170ft (9500m); range (with 66gal/300 litre drop tank, at speed quoted) 528 miles (850km).
Armament: Two MG 151/20 cannon in the wings and two MG 131 13mm heavy machine guns above engine.
History: First flight (Bf 109) May 1935, (Bf 109G) October 1941, (S 199) 1946.

When the S 199 thundered into action over an Egyptian armoured column on 29 May 1948 it caused shock and dismay to Israel's invaders, and for the first time hinted that the Jewish state might actually be able to defend itself. But in fact the S 199 was almost useless, and a far greater menace to its pilots than to its foes. It was unquestionably the worst combat aircraft built anywhere in the post-1945 era, its basic design faults further compounded by sabotage and cheating in its manufacture and numerous dangerous in-service failures.

It came about simply because in 1945 the Czechs found they had the tooling, materials and experience to continue producing the Messerschmitt Bf 109G. The S 99, almost identical to the German G-14, began to come off the assembly line in July 1945, but only two months later the entire stock of DB 605ASCM engines was destroyed when the sugar refinery in which they were stored was gutted by fire. The only alternative was to fit another engine which had originally been produced to power the He 111H bomber. Installed in the fighter airframe the Jumo 211F needed prolonged system development, but a worse shortcoming was that it ran at lower speeds and had a lower reduction-gear ratio. The result was far greater torque, passed to a propeller with broad paddle-type blades. It so accentuated the already poor takeoff and landing characteristics that the resulting fighter, designated S 199, was extremely difficult to fly, and highly dangerous to any inexperienced pilot. Swing was violent and it was common for aircraft to overturn on both takeoff and landing. Control in flight was oversensitive, and performance sluggish — achieved speed on the level hardly ever exceeded 340mph (547km/h) — and the Czechs quickly named the S 199 Mezek (Mule).

Lacking any other choice the Israelis paid $US 1·8 million on 23 April 1948 for ten of the fighters with ammunition and spares. The first was airlifted by a chartered Skymaster on 20 May 1948, the second following only a

Right: This S 199 was flown by the commander of No 101 Squadron, the Chel Ha'Avir's first fighter unit, from Herzlia in May 1948. The unit badge was painted on the nose (both sides).

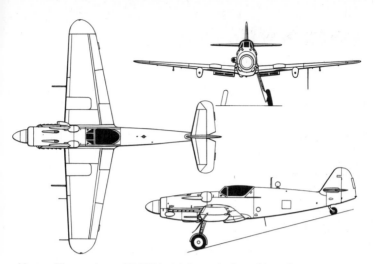

Above: Three-view of S 199 (with later design of hood).

day later; the other eight, plus a follow-on batch of 15 came in Israeli C-46s. In service the S 199 suffered extremely rapid attrition. Pulling the firing trigger caused severe swinging off-target because the two cannon gondolas hardly ever fired together; and the 13mm guns commonly shot off propeller blades, as a result of which it became standard practice to fire a brief burst soon after takeoff, towards the sea, so that a propellerless return to base could be made. Most of the S 199s were locally refitted with a rack for a bomb (in most cases a British or US 500lb [227kg] type) as well as the existing attachment and plumbing for a drop tank. A much-needed modification was to replace the Galland hood by a bulged sliding type which could be left open on takeoff or landing to allow some chance of escape for the pilot. Nothing could be done about the useless MF radio, and the fact that 101 Sqn, normally based at Herzlia, scored so many air and ground victories is a striking testimony to the very high level of skill and courage of its pilots, led until his death by Modi Alon. No Avia remained serviceable beyond May 1949.

Left: The Chel Ha'Avir S 199s had the Galland type hood, hinged to the right. This S 199 does not have the striped rudder.

Lockheed Hudson

Hudson III, Lodestar

Origin: Lockheed Aircraft Corporation, Burbank, California.
Type: Utility transport.
Engines: Two 1,200hp Wright R-1820-G205A Cyclone nine-cylinder radials. (Lodestar) two Twin Wasp or Cyclone; variant not known.
Dimensions: Span 65ft 6in (19·96m); length 44ft 4in (13·51m), (Lodestar, 49ft 10in, 15·19m); height 11ft 10½in (3·62m); wing area 551sq ft (51·19m²).
Weights (Hudson): Empty about 12,900lb (5850kg); loaded 22,360lb (10,140kg).
Performance: (Hudson) Maximum speed 260mph (418km/h); cruising speed 180–223mph (290–359km/h); service ceiling 24,500ft (7470m); range about 2,000 miles (3220km).
Armament: (Hudson, as built) two 7·7mm guns in top of nose firing ahead, two similar beam-window guns, two similar guns in Boulton Paul dorsal turret and similar gun in prone position under tail; internal bay for up to 1,400lb (635kg) various stores.
History: First flight (Hudson) 10 December 1938, (Lodestar) February 1940.

Among the less well documented aircraft of the infant Chel Ha'Avir were at least two Hudsons and a Lodestar. All were derived from the Lockheed 14 civil passenger transport of July 1937, which had had a very highly loaded wing and exceptional cruising speed, made possible by the use of area-

Consolidated PBY

PBY-5A Catalina

Origin: Consolidated-Vultee Aircraft, San Diego.
Type: Reconnaissance and air/sea rescue amphibian.
Engines: Two 1,200hp Pratt & Whitney R-1830-92 Twin Wasp 14-cylinder radials.
Dimensions: Span 104ft 0in (31·7m); length 63ft 11in (19·5m); height (on land) 20ft 2in (6·15m); wing area 1,400sq ft (130·0m²).
Weights: Empty about 20,900lb (9480kg); loaded 35,300lb (16,012kg).
Performance: Maximum speed 177mph (285km/h); cruising speed 125mph (201km/h); service ceiling 14,700ft (4481m); range 2,520 miles (4056km).
Armament: Not fitted in Israel.
History: First flight (Model 28) March 1935, (PBY-5A) November 1939.

Despite the importance of the eastern Mediterranean and Red Sea to Israel, no marine aircraft (except for the light Widgeons, see 'below) have ever been used by the Chel Ha'Avir except for rather sporadic employment of two of these wartime amphibians in 1953–59. They were historically significant in being the first ex-military aircraft ever officially sanctioned by the US government for export to Israel. Three in fact were granted licences, on the strict understanding they were unarmed (apparently Israel had no right to defend itself), but only two were actually purchased. They were among the first aircraft ever flown openly to join the Chel Ha'Avir, and during their six years of service were based at Haifa. At least during their initial service they had only HF radio and no radar.

Right: The midnight-blue PBYs had non-standard nose turrets.

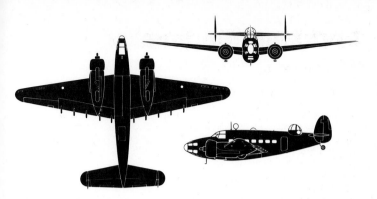

Above: Three-view of Cyclone-powered Hudson III (with turret).

increasing Fowler flaps. The military Hudson was used in large numbers by the RAF and Commonwealth with Twin Wasp or Cyclone engines, and the examples acquired by Israel were certainly ex-RAF and retained 7·7mm (0·303in) guns. In Israeli service some, at least (it is believed more than two were on strength), were flown without turrets and served at Ramat David mainly in the transport role — a curious fact, because they were efficient bombers. The lone Lodestar was one of a stretched family seating up to 18 troops and variously powered by Hornet, Twin Wasp or Cyclone engines. It was probably bought ex-US in 1948, though numerous ex-BOAC and RAF Lodestars were stored at 107 MU at Kasfareet in late 1947 pending return to the USA. None of these Lockheeds remained active by 1950.

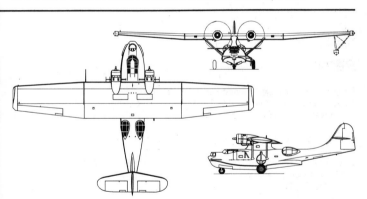

Above: Three-view of standard wartime PBY-5A amphibian.

Supermarine Spitfire
Mk IX, Mk LF.XVI (9, 16)

Origin: Supermarine Aviation Works (Vickers); built at Castle Bromwich and Woolston.
Type: Fighter-bomber.
Engine: One Rolls-Royce Merlin vee-12: (9) 1,710hp Merlin 63A, (16) 1,720hp Packard Merlin 266.
Dimensions: Span (LF) 32ft 7in (9·93m); length 31ft 3½in (9·54m); height 11ft 5in (3·48m); wing area 231sq ft (21·46m²).
Weights: Empty about 5,650lb (2563kg); loaded 7,300lb (3311kg).
Performance: Maximum speed 404mph (650km/h); initial climb 4,100ft/min (20·8m/s); service ceiling 42,000ft (12·8km); range 434 miles (698km), but see text for delivery flights.
Armament: (most) two 20mm Hispano plus four 0·303in (7·7mm) Brownings, plus 1,000lb (454kg) bombload (one 500lb [227kg] plus two 250lb [113·4kg]) or rockets; (E-type wing) as above but two 0·5in (12·7mm) in place of four 0·303in.
History: First flight 5 March 1936, (IX) 1942, (16) 1944.

Flown by dozens of Jewish pilots with the RAF during World War 2, the Spitfire was the chief weapon of Israel's enemies when the new state was born in May 1948. Indeed Spitfires of the Egyptian air force bombed and strafed Tel Aviv on the very day the British mandate expired. Against such airpower the Israelis could offer almost no defence, and the infant Chel

Below: Spitfire LF.9E with clipped wings and pointed rudder, carrying overload ferry tanks.

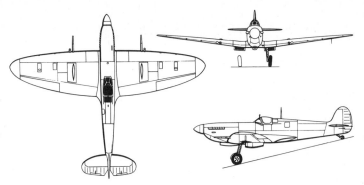

Above: Three-view of the mass-produced Spitfire IX.

Ha'Avir possessed no real fighters until the initial phase of the war had been won. But in August 1948 the answer to countless Jewish prayers suddenly emerged in distant Czechoslovakia. Perhaps to atone for the S 199s, the Czechs offered the Israelis 50 battle-worthy Spitfires!

Large numbers of Spitfires had been flown by Free Czech pilots with the RAF, and in 1945 most of them were allowed to fly their aircraft to Prague to form a new post-war air force. It is part of history that almost all officers tainted by contact with the West were arrested, and the actual post-war Czech forces were carefully assembled from loyal Communists, using Soviet weapons. Though no fewer than 76 Spitfires, all in first-class condition, were on Czech airfields, they were not permitted to be flown and the Czech

Below: Not all the Chel Ha'Avir Spitfires were of the LF (clipped-wing) variety. This example is a regular Mk IX (post-war style, Mk 9) with C-type wing and original rudder. The Spitfire was the first really effective combat aircraft possessed by the Chel Ha'Avir. The striped rudder – reminiscent of the Yak OKB's house style – did not necessarily mean 101 Sqn.

government was instructed to dispose of them. They were a mix of LF.9 and LF.16 Spitfires (in post-war arabic designations), the latter being fitted with US-built engines.

Jumping at the chance to purchase real defensive strength the Israelis signed for 50 on the spot (almost all LF. 9E type), and considered how to get the short-legged fighters to Israel. Thanks to Sam Pomerantz, one of the many *mahals* (foreign volunteers), a way was found to fly them under their own power, with everything removable stripped out and with auxiliary internal tanks plus a 90gal (409 litre) slipper belly tank. This gave enough range to cover the 1,400-mile (2253km) leg from Kunovice to Titograd (Podgorica) in southern Jugoslavia. The first six were ferried out on 24 September 1948, with the first C-54 as lead ship. All through the winter small groups of Spitfires made the dangerous flight, sometimes having to make forced landings and for one period without the Titograd refuelling stop (which demanded further auxiliary tanks which put up the weight beyond the design and stability limits).

The Chel Ha'Avir had previously assembled two Spitfires from parts salvaged from crash dumps and shot-down Egyptian Spitfires, and 101 Sqn at Herzlia had 5 aircraft by mid-October and 12 by November 1948. Nine more aircraft were purchased in 1949, followed by 30 additional Spitfires which were acquired from Italy in 1953. Altogether some 90 Spitfires in three squadrons served with the Chel Ha'Avir in 1948–55, as the backbone of the nation's air defence. The combat record shows that, largely because of the skill and experience of the pilots, they completely outfought enemy Griffon-Spitfires, Furies and jets. In 1955 the best surviving 18 were sold to Burma, and the delivery missions to that country form yet another epic story.

Above and below: The Spitfire 9E flown by Ezer Weizman, who was the third CO of 101 Squadron.

Above: Spitfire 9B (two cannon and four 0·303) parked under rare forest vegetation for machine-gun maintenance.

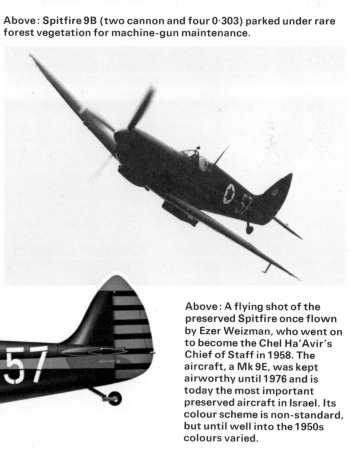

Above: A flying shot of the preserved Spitfire once flown by Ezer Weizman, who went on to become the Chel Ha'Avir's Chief of Staff in 1958. The aircraft, a Mk 9E, was kept airworthy until 1976 and is today the most important preserved aircraft in Israel. Its colour scheme is non-standard, but until well into the 1950s colours varied.

North American P-51 Mustang

P-51 D

Origin: North American Aviation, Inglewood, California.
Type: Fighter-bomber.
Engine: One 1,590hp Packard V-1650-7 (Merlin) vee-12.
Dimensions: Span 37ft 0½in (11·29m); length 32ft 3¼in (9·83m); height 13ft 8in (4·2m); wing area 233·19sq ft (21·66m²).
Weights: Empty 7,125lb (3232kg); loaded 11,600lb (5262kg).
Performance: Maximum speed 437mph (703km/h); cruising speed 240–360mph (386–579km/h); service ceiling 41,900ft (12,770m); range (internal fuel, 240mph) 950 miles (1529km), (max with drop tanks) 2,080 miles (3347km).
Armament: Six 0·50in (12·7mm) Browning guns; provision for wing racks for two stores of up to 1,000lb (454kg) each.
History: First flight (NA-73X) 26 October 1940, (P-51D) February 1944.

The North American Mustang was designed later than nearly all the other chief fighters of World War 2, and contrived by good engineering to fly faster and carry much more internal fuel without being significantly bigger or more powerful. Large numbers served in the Mediterranean theatre, but all Chel Ha'Avir examples were purchased from 1948 from distant sources. The first four, all Inglewood-built P-51Ds, were acquired from a US source in September 1948, and though it took many weeks to get them armed and fit for combat they participated in the war from the end of the year. They were the third type of fighter assigned to 101 Sqn at Herzlia, and were rated No 2 behind the Spitfires as being somewhat less agile and lacking the punch of Hispano cannon. Gradually this was seen to be a superficial assessment, and in particular the P-51's great range and endurance enabled it to fly missions beyond the reach of other fighters.

Thus, when in 1951 the Swedish Flygvåpnet put its P-51D force on the

Above: Preserved P-51D in the characteristic markings often used by No 101 Squadron.

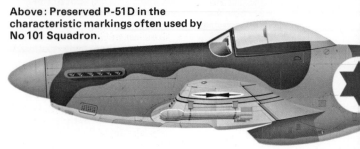

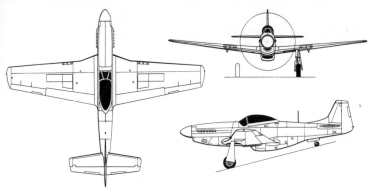

Above: Three-view of P-51D, with bomb/tank racks.

market, the Chel Ha'Avir commander, Chaim Laskov, sanctioned the purchase of 25. By this time such a deal appeared doubtful, because Israel's immediate enemies already flew jets (Egypt had both Meteors and Vampires) and the old wartime fighters were no longer able to rule the skies, even in the hands of exceptionally skilled pilots. At least the ex-Swedish Mustangs had been well maintained and in continuous front-line service, and not acquired by cloak-and-dagger methods because of laws forbidding the sale of arms to Israel. One factor in the Mustang's favour in the early 1950s was the fact that the still terribly weak Chel Ha'Avir could assimilate it and look after it. Attrition was low, and 29 were operational when the Suez war began and on 29 October 1956 were the first Israeli aircraft to go into action. They fought with distinction throughout that campaign, mainly in the ground-attack role. On their first sorties they were deliberately flown through all the Egyptian telephone lines! This caused some losses from wing and propeller damage, and at the end of the Suez war nine P-51s had been brought down. Several were purchased from Italy in 1955, and a year later all Mustangs were transferred to an OTU squadron. The purchase from Sweden was the last time the Chel Ha'Avir was forced by circumstance — this time almost wholly due to lack of money — to buy obsolescent combat aircraft.

Above: An outstanding early-1950s portrait of a P-51D with Spitfires behind. The P-51 has a non-standard gun installation and rails for 12 underwing Sura rockets.

Left: Another Chel Ha'Avir P-51D, in this case with zero-length attachments for eight British 60lb (27kg) rockets.

Bristol Beaufighter
Mk II and Mk X Mod (post-war Mk 10)

Origin: Bristol Aeroplane Company; built at Filton (II) and Weston (X).
Type: Long-range attack.
Engines: (II) two 1,280hp Rolls-Royce Merlin XX, (X, after engine change) two 1,670hp Bristol Hercules XVI 14-cylinder sleeve-valve radials.
Dimensions: Span 57ft 10in (17·63m); length 41ft 8in (12·7m); (Mk II, 42ft 9in [13m]); height 15ft 10in (4·84m); wing area 503sq ft (46·7m²).
Weights: (Mk X Mod): Empty 15,380lb (6976kg); loaded 25,400lb (11,520kg)
Performance: (Mk X Mod) Maximum speed 312mph (502km/h); cruising speed 243mph (391km/h); service ceiling 26,000ft (7925m); range 1,480 miles (2382km).
Armament: Four 20mm Hispano cannon and six 0·303in (7·7mm) machine guns; modified in Israel to carry unknown bombload.
History: First flight 17 July 1939; (X Mod) October 1947.

Whereas the immensely strong and capable Beaufighter had been one of the great and versatile war-winners of the RAF, in Israel it proved almost useless. The aircraft were acquired for hard cash in a typically circuitous manner. A company called R. Dickson and Partners bought six 'Beaus' in order to make a film about RNZAF pilots of these aircraft, on location in Scotland. One was one of the rare Merlin-powered specimens, the rest being of the post-war export model rebuilt by Fairey at Ringway with torpedo gear removed and the same mark of engine as the Beaufighter VI. The fleet

---

Grumman Widgeon
J4F-2, Model 44

Origin: Grumman Aircraft Engineering Corporation, Bethpage, NY.
Type: Light transport amphibian.
Engines: Two 200hp Ranger L-440-5 inverted-six-inline.
Dimensions: Span 40ft 0in (12·19m); length 31ft 1in (9·48m); height 11ft 5in (3·5m); wing area 245sq ft (22·76m²).
Weights: Empty 3,215lb (1458kg); loaded 4,500lb (2041kg).
Performance: Maximum speed 153mph (246km/h); cruising speed 126mph (203km/h); service ceiling 14,600ft (4450m); range 920 miles (1481km).
History: First flight (G-44) July 1940.

Below: Three-view of G-44 Widgeon.

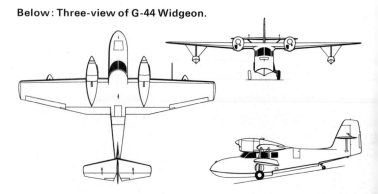

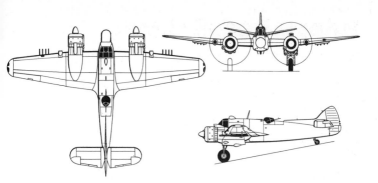

Above: Three-view of Beaufighter 10 with radar and rocket rails.

was registered G-AJMB to MG, but instead of going to Scotland headed south, one crashing at Thame, Oxford. Four staged through Corsica and after arrival in Israel were equipped with guns and ammunition acquired by even more enterprising methods. Provision was made for a bombload (under the wings) and contemporary accounts speak of a crew of three, the regular pilot and observer being accompanied by a bombardier (there was no way in which a bombsight could have been installed except in the rear fuselage). One Beau was cannibalised for spares and the other three made a few combat missions with 103 Sqn from Ramat David, but suffered appalling serviceability. On 20 October 1948 one was shot down in Egypt and the crew (numbering three) were tortured to death. All Beaufighter operations ceased by November.

The G-44 light commercial amphibian served with many operators, civil and military, even though barely 200 in all were built. Two were acquired ex-military for Israel in late 1948; there is some evidence they were ex-USN J4F-2s though similar machines served the USAAF, RN, RCAF and many Allied nations. Of tough all-metal construction, and with main gears that actually retracted instead of merely being cranked up for water landings, the Widgeon was a trim and quite popular machine which, almost alone among Israeli types, could alight on the country's inland lakes as well as airfields. The cockpit seated two pilots, and the main cabin could seat three passengers but in the Chel Ha'Avir was usually used for cargo. One of the few snags apart from difficulty with spares was rather poor engine reliability. Both Widgeons crashed, one on land and the other, fatally, into Lake Tiberius.

Below: Wreckage of one of the Israeli Widgeons. This is believed to have been the one that crashed into Lake Tiberius, killing Canadian fighter pilot (Mahal volunteer) Ralph Moster.

Douglas DC-5

DC-5 (C-110)

Origin: Douglas Aircraft Company, Santa Monica; design and manufacture at El Segundo.
Type: Transport.
Engines: Two 1,100hp Wright GR-1820-G102A Cyclone nine-cylinder radials.
Dimensions: Span 78ft 0in (23·77m); length 62ft 1in (18·92m); height 19ft 10in (6·045m); wing area 824sq ft (76·55m²).
Weights: Empty 13,674lb (6203kg); loaded 21,000lb (9526kg).
Performance: Maximum speed 259mph (417km/h); cruising speed 203mph (327km/h); service ceiling 22,400ft (6828m); range 1,600 miles (2575km).
History: First flight February 1939.

Developed at the Navy plant at El Segundo under Ed Heinemann, the DC-5 was started in 1938 as a transport outgrowth of the DB-7 bomber. Carrying up to 22 passengers or troops and available with a large side cargo door, it was far more useful than the DC-3 in having a level floor at low level, as well as a markedly higher performance on similar power. Tragically General Hap Arnold told Heinemann to stop the programme, as the Army had decided to buy only the C-47. Nevertheless 12 DC-5s were built, including R3Ds

---

Boeing-Stearman Kaydet

PT-17

Origin: Boeing Airplane, Stearman Aircraft Division, Wichita, Kansas.
Type: Primary pilot trainer.
Engine: One 220hp Continental R-670-5 seven-cylinder radial.
Dimensions: Span 32ft 2in (9·80m); length (typical) 24ft 9½in (7·56m); height 9ft 8in (2·95m); wing area 298sq ft (27·69m²).
Weights: Empty 1,931lb (876kg); loaded 2,635lb (1195kg).
Performance: Maximum speed 135mph (217km/h); cruising speed 96mph (154km/h); service ceiling 13,200ft (4023m); range 395 miles (636km).
History: First flight (Model 75) early 1936.

Below: Three-view of typical Boeing Stearman trainer.

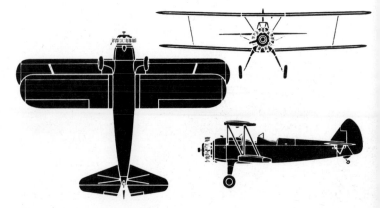

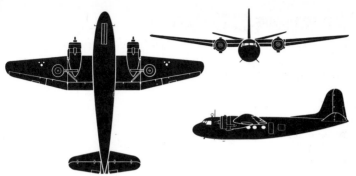

Above: Three-view of DC-5 (*Bagel Lancer* had D/F acorn above cockpit).

for the Marines and C-110s for the Army. One of the latter served with KLM and KNILM, 31 Sqn RAAF, Pan American, ANA and New Holland Airways before, in June 1948, passing in Sicily to the Chel Ha'Avir. Described as "a flying scrap-heap", she faithfully shuttled troops and supplies into the Negev and on occasion served as a bomber, the stores being rolled out of the door. At the end of the war this famous and almost legendary machine, locally called the *Bagel Lancer*, was pensioned off to the Tel Aviv aviation school, but sadly she was scrapped there in 1955.

In 1933, while the giant United Aircraft and Transport combine was still being dismembered by Federal edict, Stearman flew the Model 70 training biplane. After long delays it led to the chief biplane trainer of the USAAF, the Kaydet, made in various sub-types to the tune of 10,346. Several thousand were sold as surplus in the post-war era, and 20 were purchased in the USA at the end of 1948 and shipped to Israel dismantled, as 'spare parts'. More Kaydets arrived after the lifting of the sales embargo. They were used for pilot training and general utility duties. They proved extremely trouble-free and popular, but after 1955 they were increasingly replaced in the flight schools and passed to civilian uses, several being modified for agricultural purposes. One is still flying privately in Israel.

Below: One of the original batch of 20 PT-17s with camouflaged sides and upper surfaces. In the 1950s, when perhaps 50 were in use, the usual colour was yellow overall.

Airspeed Consul

A.S.65

Origin: Airspeed Ltd, Portsmouth.
Type: Crew trainer and light transport.
Engines: Two 395hp Armstrong Siddeley Cheetah 10 seven-cylinder radials.
Dimensions: Span 53ft 4in (16·26m); length 35ft 4in (10·77m); height 10ft 1½in (3·09m); wing area 348sq ft (32·33m²).
Weights: Empty 6,047lb (2743kg); loaded 8,250lb (3742kg).
Performance: Maximum speed 190mph (306km/h); cruising speed 146mph (235km/h); service ceiling 19,000ft (5790m); range 900 miles (1448km).
History: First flight (Oxford) June 1937, (Consul) December 1945.

Finding itself with large numbers of part-finished Oxford trainers, on contracts cancelled at the end of World War 2, Airspeed sensibly produced a simple civilian version which was certificated by 15 March 1946 and put on the market at £5,500. It sold readily, the standard machine having the pilot on the left of the cockpit, a radio operator or navigator on the right and a five-seat cabin arranged with two seats at the front, one seat on the right (opposite the door) and a two-seat bench at the rear. About 18 were leased by British charter operators to the UN commission in Palestine before the British withdrawal, and most of these were bought by the Chel Ha'Avir after the armistice of March 1949. They subsequently served until 1957 as the standard multi-engine-pilot, radio and navigation trainer, and also filled in as light transports. They were among the few popular and trouble-free types used in the tough early days, but most survivors were withdrawn in 1958–59.

DHC-1 Chipmunk

DHC-1B-1, Chipmunk T.10

Origin: de Havilland Aircraft of Canada, Downsview, and DH Aircraft, Hatfield/Chester.
Type: Primary trainer.
Engine: One DH Gipsy Major inverted-four-inline, (B-1) 140hp Mk IC, (T.10) 145hp Mk 8.
Dimensions: Span 34ft 4in (10·46m); length 25ft 8in (7·82m); height 7ft 1in (2·16m); wing area 172sq ft (15·98m²).

Below: Three-view of British-built Chipmunk T.10.

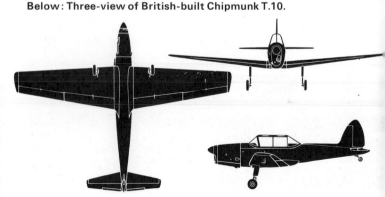

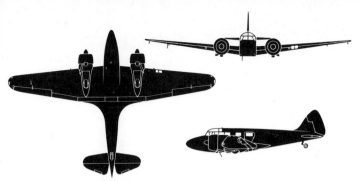

Above: Three-view of Airspeed Consul.

Below: Possibly at Hatzerim, two of the Consuls used for twin-engine training stand next to a line-up of Harvards.

Weights: (UK T.10) empty 1,417lb (643kg); loaded 2,000lb (907kg).
Performance: Maximum speed 138mph (222km/h); cruising speed 119mph (191·5km/h); service ceiling 16,000ft (4877m); range 300 miles (483km).
History: First flight 22 May 1946.

The familiar Chipmunk, the neat stressed-skin tandem trainer designed in Canada as the heir to the Tiger Moth, is one of the many puzzles of the early equipment of the Chel Ha'Avir. Only one of the initial Canadian batch was acquired, not later than May 1949, and this only remained in service for a short period. The type was not particularly popular and was considered to have a poor field performance in summer.

Below: Allegedly Canadian-built, this Chipmunk had the UK canopy.

49

Miles M.57 Aerovan

Aerovan 4

Origin: Miles Aircraft Ltd, Woodley, Reading.
Type: Utility transport.
Engines: Two 155hp Blackburn Cirrus Major 3 inverted 4-inline.
Dimensions: Span 50ft 0in (15·24m); length 36ft (10·97m); height 13ft 6in (4·1m); wing area 390sq ft (36·23m²).
Weights: Empty 3,000lb (1361kg); maximum loaded 5,800lb (2631kg).
Performance: Maximum speed 127mph (204km/h); cruising speed 112mph (180km/h); service ceiling 13,250ft (4039m); range with maximum payload 400 miles (644km).
History: First flight (Aerovan 1) 26 January 1945, (Mk 4) 1946.

Typical of the products of the small Miles company in being developed quickly and cheaply to fulfil useful tasks, the Aerovan was really a lightplane yet had a cargo hold big enough to take a small car, which could be driven on board via the opened rear of the main pod section of the fuselage. Construction was of wood, and despite the lack of power STOL performance was assisted by Miles auxiliary-aerofoil flaps. In temperate climates it was possible to carry one long ton (1016kg) of cargo or eight passengers out of the smallest fields, and by late 1947 Aerovans were serving in many countries. Two are said to have reached South Africa, from where they were transferred to the Chel Ha'Avir in 1948. Their problems were poor performance on a hot day and inability of the wooden structure to withstand the tough environment, but otherwise their unique trucking capability was much appreciated.

Right: Though one report states two Aerovans were obtained from South Africa, this Aerovan 4 had previously borne British registration (it is painted over but appears under the wing to have been G-AJWI). This particular Aerovan led a charmed life until it was destroyed by enemy action on 17 July 1948.

Temco Buckaroo

TE-1A, T-35

Origin: Texas Engineering & Manufacturing, Dallas.
Type: Primary trainer.
Engine: One 145hp Continental C145-2H six-cylinder opposed.
Dimensions: Span 29ft 2in (8·89m); length 21ft 8in (6·6m); height 6ft 1½in (1·87m); wing area 134sq ft (12·45m²).
Weights: Empty 1,301lb (590kg); loaded 1,840lb (834·6kg).
Performance: Maximum speed 160mph (257·5km/h); cruising speed 136mph (219km/h); service ceiling 14,000ft (4267m); range 470 miles (756km).
History: First flight 1949.

In 1947 Temco took over the assets of Globe Aircraft, and one of its first actions was to develop the successful Globe Swift into a military trainer with tandem seating under a long canopy with sliding hoods. The resulting TE-1A Buckaroo was a good all-metal machine with appreciably lower costs than the rival Beech Mentor. Three, designated T-35, were tested by the USAF but lost out to the T-34 Mentor, partly because of the tailwheel landing gear. A contract was placed, however, for ten production machines (53-4465/4474) and these appear to have been split equally between Saudi Arabia and

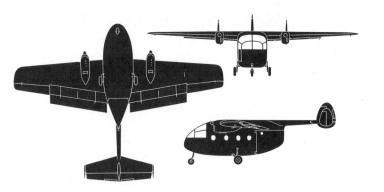

Above: Three-view of Miles M.57 Aerovan 4.

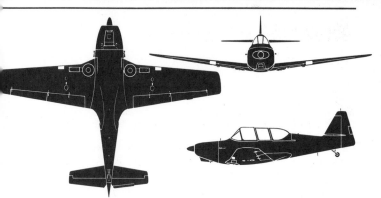

Above: Three-view of TE-1A Buckaroo.

Israel. The five supplied to the Chel Ha'Avir proved quite popular, and on the same power offered performance considerably higher than that of the Chipmunk, and also slightly greater aerobatic capability. Why the US government should have given these aircraft to Israel and an Arab nation is unexplained, especially as five is too few for effective use and merely complicates the training, maintenance and spares problem. After evaluating the Buckaroo, the Chel Ha'Avir chose the Fokker S.11.

Nord Norécrin

N.1203/II

Origin: SNCA du Nord, Paris.
Type: Light cabin monoplane.
Engine: One 135hp Régnier 4LO inverted 4-inline.
Dimensions: Span 33ft 6⅓in (10·22m); length 23ft 7⅞in (7·21m); height 9ft 5¾in (2·89m); wing area 186·2sq ft (17·3m²).
Weights: Empty 1,437lb (652kg); maximum loaded 2,315lb (1050kg).
Performance: Maximum speed 174mph (280km/h); cruising speed 137mph (220km/h); service ceiling 16,400ft (5km); range 559 miles (900km).
History: First flight (N.1200) 15 December 1945, (N.1203/II) 1948.

During World War 2 the French Nord group made 285 Messerschmitt Bf 108 Taifuns, developed the Me 208 and produced its own version of the latter as the N.1101 Ramier (military) and Noralpha (civil). From the latter stemmed the N.1200 three-seat cabin machine with Renault 4-Pei engine, in turn becoming the N.1203 production type with the cheaper Regnier. Altogether 470 of these all-metal machines were delivered to many private and official customers, the 1203/II being a four-seater. Features included large flaps and retractable tricycle landing gear, but in the late 1940s a spate of structural failures led to important airframe modifications. Two Norécrins were bought from France and used as ambulances.

Right: Still not a fully developed type, the two Norécrins had a hard life flying front-line casevac missions from late 1948.

Fokker S.11

S.11 Instructor

Origin: NV Nederlandsche Vliegtuigenfabriek Fokker, Amsterdam.
Type: Primary trainer.
Engine: One 190hp Lycoming O-435-A six-cylinder opposed.
Dimensions: Span 36ft 1in (11·00m); length 26ft 9⅔in (8·17m); height 7ft 10½in (2·40m); wing area 199·1sq ft (18·5m²).
Weights: Empty 1,775lb (805kg); loaded 2,425lb (1100kg).
Performance: Maximum speed 130mph (209km/h); cruising speed 102mph (164km/h); service ceiling 12,630ft (3850m); range 398 miles (640km).
History: First flight 18 December 1947.

As soon as the initial war for survival had been concluded by the spring 1949 armistices, the Chel Ha'Avir began to consider its future equipment. Though most of its so-called front-line combat aircraft were really lightplanes, it still lacked a modern trainer, designed from the start for military pupil pilots. It was a major feather in Fokker's hat when the S.11, designed and built in a new factory that replaced the one destroyed and looted during the war, was selected as the standard Chel Ha'Avir primary trainer. It had adequate performance, no shortcomings, room for a third seat for a pupil to watch the side-by-side pupil and instructor in front, and a reasonable price. The first S.11 arrived in Israel in December 1949. Forty more were ordered and delivered by sea in 1951. These aircraft served in the flying school until mid-1953 and were then transferred to the light transport squadron since it was decided that the Kaydet was a better trainer. The last ten surviving S.11s were sold to civil operators at the end of 1954.

Above: Three-view of standard Nord 1203 Norécrin.

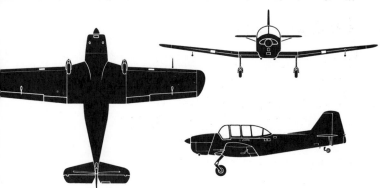

Above: Three-view of Fokker S.11 Instructor.

Below: The S.11 fleet at the Chel Ha'Avir Flying School were painted yellow. They were replaced by PT-17s and PA-18-150s.

DH Mosquito
DH.98, Mks T.3, FB.6, PR.16, NF.30, TR.33

Origin: de Havilland Aircraft, Hatfield; built at Standard Motors, Canley (several of the Mk VI, called Mk 6 post-war).

Type: (VI) fighter/bomber, (16) photo reconnaissance.

Engines: Two Rolls-Royce Merlin vee-12, (VI) 1,635hp Mk 25, (16) 1,710hp Mk 77.

Dimensions: Span 54ft 2in (16·5m); length (VI) 41ft 2in (12·55m), (16) 40ft 6in (12·34m); height 15ft 3½in (4.66m); wing area 454sq ft (42·18m²).

Weights: Empty (VI) typical 13,800lb (6260kg), (16) about 16,200lb (7348kg); loaded (VI with 42gal, 191 litre drop tanks) 21,020lb (9535kg), (16 with 100gal, 455 litre drop tanks) 23,630lb (10,719kg).

Performance: Maximum speed (VI) 368mph (592km/h), (16) 419mph (674km/h); cruising speed (typical, either) 220mph (354km/h); service ceiling (VI) 26,000ft (7925m), (16) 35,000ft (10,670m); range (VI, max cruise) 960 miles (1545km), (16) 1,490 miles (2398km).

Armament: (VI) four 20mm and four 0·303in guns firing ahead; two 250lb (113kg) bombs in bomb bay plus two 500lb (227kg) bombs or eight rockets or various other stores on underwing racks; (16) as built, none.

History: First flight (DH.98) November 1940; (VI) June 1942, (16) July 1943.

Famed as 'The Wooden Wonder', the Mosquito was planned as an unarmed bomber and reconnaissance aircraft but was so outstanding a design that it proliferated into 39 marks for many purposes. The most numerous was the FB.6, which combined the guns of the fighters with at least part of the offensive load of the bombers, and was widely used for ground attack and anti-shipping missions in World War 2. A single PR.16 arrived in Israel from Britain in July 1948 (a second aircraft of the same version crashed on its way to Israel). In February 1951 the IAF signed a contract with France to purchase 59 Mosquitos of the fighter version (mostly FB.6 but including a few NF.30 night fighters), four PR.16s and three T.3 trainers. Two additional Mk 6 were bought from Nord Aviation. These aircraft were flown to Israel between June 1951 and May 1952. The night fighters were fitted in Israel with APS-4 radar, and in 1953 formed the first NF squadron. Fourteen TR.33 Mosquitos were purchased from the Royal Navy in 1954–55. They were refurbished by Eagle Aviation and flown to Israel (one of these was TW238). The FB.6 remained the chief Israeli long-range attack aircraft from 1953 to 1956, although the wooden airframe gave prolonged serious difficulty arising mainly from distortion and the failure of adhesive joints. The Mosquitos were retired from active service after seeing action in the 1956 Sinai Campaign.

At a late date, in summer 1956 when the Mosquito was no longer safe in MiG-filled skies, three PR.16s were flown out openly with Israeli civil markings from Hurn, England. They had been NS742, RG174 and TA614 of the Royal Navy, and were completely refurbished as photographic machines which gave excellent service in Israel until at least 1960 (at least one continued in the 1960s as a civil geophysical survey aircraft).

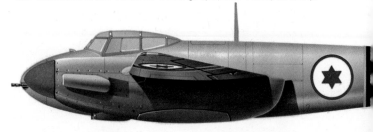

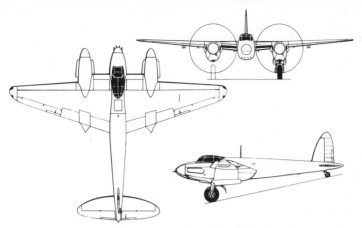

Above: Three-view of Mosquito Mk 6 with underwing bomb racks.

Above: Though the Chel Ha'Avir purchased only PR.16s these Mk 16s have become bombers with bomb doors and wing racks.

Above: Taken at an Armée de l'Air base in 1951 this photo shows Israeli ferry pilots collecting ex-French Mosquito Mk 6 fighter/bombers.

Left: The Mk 6 was by far the most numerous Mosquito model flown by the Chel Ha'Avir.

Gloster Meteor
Meteor T.7, F.8, FR.9 and NF.13

Origin: Gloster Aircraft, Gloucester; (13) Armstrong Whitworth Aircraft, Coventry.

Type: (7) dual trainer, (8) day fighter, (9) fighter/reconnaissance, (13) night interceptor.

Engines: Two Rolls-Royce Derwent turbojets, (7, early 8 and most 9) 3,500lb (1588kg) Derwent 8, (late 8, some 9 and 13 on delivery) Derwent 8 cleared to 3,650lb (1656kg) with larger inlets.

Dimensions: Span (7, 8, 9) 37ft 2in (11·33m), (13) 43ft 0in (13·1m); length (8) 44ft 7in (13·59m), (7, 9) 43ft 6in (13·26m), (13) 48ft 6in (14·78m); height (8, 13) 13ft 10in (4·22m), (7, 9) 13ft 8in (4·17m); wing area (7, 8, 9) 350sq ft (32·5m²), (13) 374sq ft (34·75m²).

Weights: Empty (8) 10,626lb (4820kg), (9) 10,891lb (4940kg), (13) 12,393lb (5621kg); loaded (clean) (8) 15,700lb (7122kg), (9) 15,785lb (7160kg), (13) 18,888lb (8568kg); loaded (max) (8) 19,100lb (8664kg), (9) 19,355lb (8779kg), (13) 20,490lb (9294kg).

Performance: Maximum speed (8, 9 at 10,000ft, 3·05km) 595mph (958km/h), (13 at 9842ft, 3km) 579mph (932km/h); service ceiling (8, 9) 44,000ft (13·4km), (13) 43,000ft (13·11km); range (internal fuel) (8, 9) 690 miles (1110km), (13) 720 miles (1159km).

Armament: (7) provision for eight rockets; (8, 9) four 20mm guns in nose, eight underwing rocket attachments; (13) four 20mm guns in wings.

History: First flight (F.9/40) March 1943, (8) October 1948, (9) March 1950, (13) December 1952.

Though crude and often uncomfortable, the Meteor had a good all-round performance by the standards of the late 1940s, and large numbers were sold to many air forces. Advantages included tough all-metal construction and systems which, though often needing maintenance, differed in only trivial details from those of familiar wartime types and could readily be looked after

Above: Gloster had to design and test ground-attack armament at its own expense on the PV "Reaper" Meteor. Thus it was ready for the Chel Ha'Avir Meteor 8 fighter and attack aircraft.

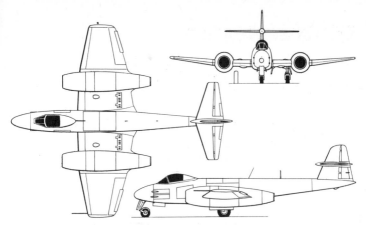

Above: Three-view of Gloster Meteor 8 without external load.

by units with limited resources. Another asset was a relatively low price, and this was of prime importance when in spring 1953 Britain lifted the embargo on exports of war material to Middle East countries. Israel purchased 11 Meteor F.8 fighters and four T.7 trainers, all basically to RAF standard but modified after delivery with eight pairs of underwing bolt-holes and electrical sockets for air/ground rockets (usually the American 5in HVAR). In 1954 seven FR.9s were purchased; this variant, essentially an F.8 with a pilot-controlled reconnaissance camera aimed obliquely ahead or laterally in the nose, had since 1950 served with the RAF in Egypt and filled a long-standing gap in the Chel Ha'Avir. Two ex-Belgian T.7s arrived in 1957.

Another and equally serious gap was filled in 1955 by the purchase of six Armstrong Whitworth Meteor NF.13 (ex-RAF) night fighters. These had the old AI Mk 10 radar but at least could do some kind of interception job by night, and also had a Godfrey cold-air unit for cockpit conditioning. They remained in front-line service until after 1960.

Above: The preserved NF.13 has Service Number 157 and a winged 6 on its nose.

Below: A local modification to the Mk 8 Meteors was fitting a rear-view canopy.

Nord Noratlas

N.2501IS

Origin: SNCA du Nord, Paris; licence-manufacture by Flugzeugbau Nord (Weser, Hamburger and Siebelwerke ATG), West Germany.
Type: Airlift transport.
Engines: Two 2,040hp SNECMA-built Bristol Hercules 739 14—cylinder sleeve-valve radials.
Dimensions: Span 106ft 7in (32·5m); length 71ft 10in (21·89m); height 20ft 6in (6·25m); wing area 1,089sq ft (101·2m²).
Weights: Empty 28,825lb (13,075kg); loaded 50,705lb (23,000kg).
Performance: Maximum speed 273mph (440km/h); cruising speed 208mph (335km/h); service ceiling 24,600ft (7500m); range (max fuel, reduced payload) 1,864 miles (3000km).
Armament: None.
History: First flight (N.2500) September 1949, (2501) November 1950.

In the immediate post-war era France produced a plethora of prototype aircraft, nearly all of which vanished without trace. One of those that made good was the Nord 2500, a cargo transport with the same twin-boom configuration as the American C-119, with the cockpit in the nose of a capacious nacelle. Like the US type, the rear doors were of the left/right clamshell type, so for air-dropping heavy loads they had to be removed before takeoff, causing turbulence and high drag. Despite this, the more powerful 2501 proved an excellent aircraft, produced in large numbers in France and Germany in a programme that led directly to the Transall, produced by the same partners, designed in 1959 and flown in 1962. Israel bought eight N.2501IS direct from Nord in 1955–59, a further 12 from Germany in 1962, and four more later. The first, 4X-FAP, was delivered before the end of 1955, and immediately proved extremely popular and capable. In the Suez war the French-built aircraft flew round the clock, in particular air-dropping all the supplies needed by the fast-moving columns in the Sinai. Another role was target-towing. The entire force operated with conspicuous success until 1976 when this type was retired; six were sold to the Hellenic Air Force 355th Sqn.

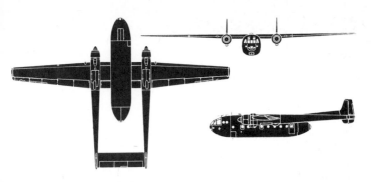

Above: Three-view of Nord 2501 Noratlas.

Above: 4X-FAU as an uncamouflaged Israeli N.2501IS awaiting collection in France (note "Super DC-3" in rear).

Below: After delivery the aircraft were camouflaged and painted with national insignia but retained civil registration.

Dassault Ouragan

MD.450

Origin: Avions Marcel Dassault, Paris.
Type: Fighter/bomber.
Engine: One 5,070lb (2300kg) thrust Hispano-Suiza Nene 104B turbojet (Rolls-Royce licence).
Dimensions: Span (over tanks) 43ft 2in (13·16m); length 35ft 2¾in (10·74m); height 13ft 7in (4·14m); wing area 256·2sq ft (23·8m²).
Weights: Empty 9,131lb (4142kg); normal loaded (tip tanks plus 16 rockets) 16,323lb (7404kg).
Performance: Maximum speed (clean, sea level) 584mph (940km/h); cruising speed (max) 460mph (740km/h); service ceiling 42,650ft (13km); range (max with tip tanks) 572 miles (920km).
Armament: Four 20mm Hispano 404 guns; wing attachments for 16 rockets or two 1,000lb (454kg) bombs (not affecting carriage of tip tanks).
History: First flight February 1949.

The best of the vast crop of French early jet fighters, the MD.450 of 1949 was an extremely simple but well-engineered machine which entered service with no major problems and led to the greatest series of combat aircraft produced in Western Europe since 1945. Though straight-winged, and in many respects inferior to the contemporary F-84G (let alone an F-86 or MiG-15), the Ouragan was easy to fly accurately, a steady gun platform and good in the ground-attack role. Production aircraft became available from December 1951, and a large export order was placed by India (previously in the pocket of Britain) in 1953. Israel was at this time trying to emulate the RAF and obtain 24 Sabres from Canada, but under US pressure Canadair Ltd

Above: This Ouragan has zero-length launchers for eight rockets instead of bomb racks. The adjacent C-47 has the original tailwheel.

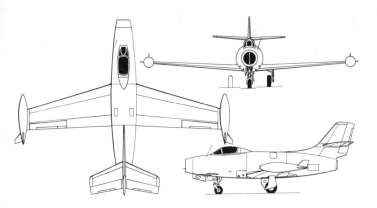

Above: Three-view of MD.450 Ouragan without racks or pylons.

declined to proceed to a contract. This almost drove Israel into the arms of Dassault. For the longer term a major contract for an advanced Mystère was negotiated, and 24 Ouragans were bought as a stop-gap in January 1955. In the event the Ouragan proved more than a temporary expedient, a further 51 (42+9) being supplied ex-Armée de l'Air, making 75 in all by 1957. In the Suez war some 20 Ouragans flew intensively and with notable success in close-support missions, causing havoc among Egyptian armour and even wrecking a destroyer escort (ex-RN *Hunt* class). The Ouragan proved almost able to dogfight a MiG-15 when flown by a skilled pilot (unlike a Meteor), and not one was lost in air combat in the Suez war. Altogether 51 participated in the 1967 war. They were retired in January 1973, and 18 were sold to El Salvador in 1975.

Above: This Ouragan is the same as that on the facing page, but here it has four rail-type rocket launchers flanking pylons for two 1,000lb (454kg) bombs.

Left: After the haphazard early years the Chel Ha'Avir combat aircraft by 1953 had organized insignia and unit markings. Even today security on units remains absolute.

61

Dassault Mystère

Mystère IVA

Origin: Avions Marcel Dassault, Paris.
Type: Fighter/bomber.
Engine: One 7,716lb (3500kg) Hispano-Suiza Verdon 350 turbojet (based on Rolls-Royce Tay).
Dimensions: Span 36ft 5¾in (11·12m); length 42ft 2in (12·85m); height 15ft 1in (4·6m); wing area 344·4sq ft (32·0m²).
Weights: Empty 12,950lb (5874kg); loaded (max with bombs plus tanks) 20,944lb (9500kg).
Performance: Maximum speed (clean, sea level) 696mph (1120km/h); cruising speed 488mph (785km/h); service ceiling 49,200ft (15km); range (internal fuel) 572 miles (920km).
Armament: Two 30mm DEFA 551 guns; four wing pylons theoretically all able to carry a 1,000lb (454kg) bomb or assorted rocket pods but two usually occupied by tanks.
History: First flight (IV) September 1952.

Always keeping one eye on what North American Aviation was doing, Dassault's design staff at St Cloud pressed ahead at a furious pace from 1951 onwards, perpetually producing prototypes incorporating one or two minor or major improvements but seldom involving much risk. The Mystère II introduced more powerful engines and modestly swept wings and tail, and the Mystère IV took the process further with increased sweep and reduced wing and tail thickness, at the cost of tapered and stretched plates machined on giant skin mills to cover the wings. Flight controls were fully powered, landing gear redesigned, a spine added from cockpit to fin and the tailplane made a primary control surface, as in the F-86E Sabre, the elevators becoming hinged surfaces to increase camber. Large numbers were ordered, including 225 paid for by American Off-Shore Procurement, and Armée de l'Air examples reached EC12 at Cambrai in late 1954 (many saw action at Suez). The Israeli order of January 1955 included 60 Mystère IVAs, essen-

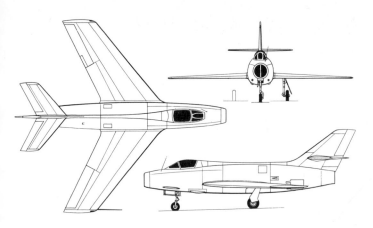

Above: Three-view of Dassault Mystère IVA without stores.

tially identical to those for the French and Indians. Deliveries began shortly before the Suez war and the sixteen then in operational service with the Chel Ha'Avir distinguished themselves in air combat to a remarkable degree, generally proving (in Israel's opinion) superior to any of the Arab MiG fighters. Used mainly for top cover they destroyed a MiG-17, three MiG-15s and four Vampires without loss, though one Mystère succumbed to ground fire. From 1962 they moved to the surface-attack role, eight being lost in the 1967 war. All were withdrawn in February 1971.

Left: Carrying drop tanks of 137gal (623-lit) size (larger tanks of 181·5gal were an option) this Mystère IVA does not have its Service Number repeated in black on the fin, though it has a unit badge.

Below: Towing a Mystère IVA with no stores pylons of any kind, but with its airbrakes hanging open. These aircraft were beautifully built and nice to fly but woe betide a landing slower than 260km/h!

SNCASO Vautour

SO.4050 Vautour IIA, IIBR and II.1N(E)

Origin: SNCA du Sud-Ouest (SNCASO), Paris (later styled Sud-Aviation, today Aérospatiale).

Type: (IIA) bomber, (II.1N/E) electronic warfare.

Engines: Two 7,716lb (3500kg) SNECMA Atar 101E-3 turbojets.

Dimensions: Span 49ft 6in (15·08m); length (A) 51ft 1in (15·5m), (1N/E) 51ft 11in (15·82m); height 14ft 2in (4·32m); wing area 484·4sq ft (45m²).

Weights: (A) Empty 24,030lb (10,900kg); loaded 44,092lb (20,000kg).

Performance:(A) Maximum speed 690 mph (1110km/h) at sea level; cruising speed 550mph (885km/h); service ceiling (new) 49,200ft (15km); range 1,900 miles (3058km) (max ferry with drop tanks, 3,700 miles, 5954km).

Armament: (A) four 30mm DEFA 553 guns, internal bombload of up to three 1,000lb (454kg) or six 750lb (340kg), plus underwing load of up to four 1,000lb (454kg), normal maximum being 5,300lb (2404kg).

History: First flight (SO.4050) October 1952, (IIA) April 1956.

One of the really outstanding aircraft produced in the early jet era by French designers, the SO.4050 was midway in size between traditional fighters and light twin-engined bombers, and, with twin axial engines and fully swept wings and tail, it exceeded the speed of sound in a shallow dive. Numerous prototypes explored three chief variations, out of 14 projected variants, and though nothing like the planned number were built, the Vautour proved an excellent machine and gave long and satisfactory service to France and Israel. The principal Israeli version, the IIA, was a single-seater, unlike all the other production models. A tactical attack machine, it combined the guns of the IIN (later II.1N) night fighter with the heavy offensive load of the IIB

Above: This preserved EW-dedicated Vautour (the eighth IIN) has the same winged-6 nose insignia as the Meteor NF.13.

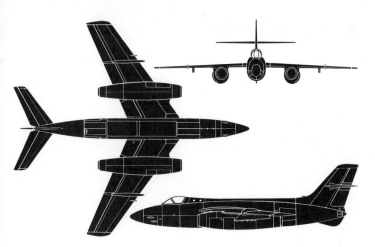

Above: Three-view of Vautour IIA.

bomber, but bombs were aimed by the pilot in shallow dives, using a depressed-reticle mode on the gunsight, instead of having a bombardier in a glazed nose. France ordered 300 of this version and production aircraft were available by mid-1957, but the order was terminated at 30 and none was delivered. Israel promptly closed a deal for 18 at a most favourable price and found it had a real winner (it had opened negotiations much earlier).

In service from August 1957 the 18 Vautour IIAs proved tough and reliable, and unlike the much larger B-47, the French machine did not prove especially tricky to land on its bicycle landing gear. Unlike the French Vautours, the Chel Ha'Avir aircraft were camouflaged and normally operated with under-wing tanks. Electronics were several times updated.

Above: One of the four Vautour IIBR recon-bombers, with a multi-sensor pallet in the weapons bay. This one is carrying training Sidewinder AAMs.

Left: The IIA was used chiefly for attack missions, night fighting being very rare. This aircraft lacks the medal ribbon often seen under the Vautour tail badge.

Altogether the Chel Ha'Avir purchased a total of about 30 Vautours in three versions. These comprised at least 18 IIAs delivered in 1957–58; four IIBRs with multi-sensor installations for reconnaissance missions (three arriving in 1960 and a fourth later after one of the original three was lost); and eight IIN night fighters, seven being acquired in 1957–58 and one in 1966. The eighth IIN had a long, pointed nose and was fitted for EW roles. It bore the name 'Phantomas' on its nose and the number 70. This was the only Vautour used for EW missions. All other IIA and IIN Vautours were used for bombing and attack missions, and saw active duty until after the War of Attrition, which ended in August 1970. Four Vautours had been lost in the 1967 war, and at the beginning of 1972 all remaining Vautours were retired.

Left: Silhouettes of two II-28s, two MiG-17s and two MiG-21s on the fin of this IIA represent ground-attack targets destroyed.

Below: Tail badges and two of the three Service Numbers have been censored in this echelon of two II.1Ns and (furthest) a IIA.

Fouga Magister
CM.170

Origin: Etablissments Fouga, Béziers, later Potez-Air Fouga, later Aéro-spatiale; licence-built by Bedek, later IAI, Lod, Israel.

Type: Trainer and light attack.

Engines: Two 880lb (400kg) Turboméca Marboré IIA turbojets, later replaced by 1,058lb (480kg) Marboré VI.

Dimensions: Span (over tanks) 39ft 10in (12·15m); length 33ft 0in (10·06m); height 9ft 2in (2·80m); wing area 186·2sq ft (17·3m²).

Weights: Empty 4,740lb (2150kg); loaded (no tip tanks) 6,283lb (2850kg), (max) 7,055lb (3200kg).

Performance: Maximum speed 404mph (650km/h) at sea level, 444mph (715km/h) at 30,000ft (9144m); service ceiling 36,000ft (11km); range (30,000ft/9144m, tip tanks, 26gal/120 litre reserve) 575 miles (925km).

Armament: Two 7·62mm (0·3in) guns in nose; underwing racks for two 110lb (50kg) bombs, or two AS.11 missiles or two pods each for 18 rockets of 37mm calibre or various other light stores.

History: First flight July 1952; production aircraft February 1956 and Israeli assembled aircraft July 1960.

From the mid-1950s Bedek Aviation (today Israel Aircraft Industries) dreamed of manufacturing aircraft. After long planning the decision was taken in December 1956 to construct the French Fouga CM.170 Magister light jet trainer. Of stressed-skin construction, and distinguished by its long-span wings, butterfly (V-type) tail and extremely short landing gear, the tandem-seat Magister had higher performance than most jet trainers and was cleared to carry weapons and fly light attack missions. It had been widely adopted by NATO air forces and was going into production in West Germany by Heinkel and Messerschmitt, later linked in Flugzeug-Union Süd. It took immense efforts to create a national aircraft industry from scratch, and to begin with Bedek imported airframe portions and all other items from France. The factory at Lod had to grow quickly and learn many new skills and some 109 engineering changes were incorporated at Chel Ha'Avir request, one being a switch to manual ailerons of increased area. The first locally assembled Magister was handed over on 7 July 1960, when Bedek became IAI. Bet-Shemesh Engines took on production of the Marboré from 1969. Airframe production began in 1962, 16 sets of parts being supplied from France and numerous wing-sets coming from Heinkel to make up for IAI being unable to deliver wings on time. By 1967 forty-five Magisters were in

Above: Israel Aircraft Industries cut its teeth with the Magister, introducing many structural and systems changes and clearing a variety of fits for weapons not seen previously on this type. This typical example served with the Chel Ha'Avir school at Hatzerim.

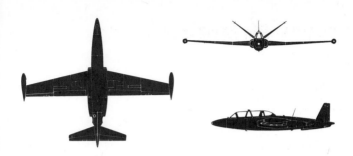

Above: Three-view of basic CM.170 Magister.

use in the Six-Day War and they were intensively used on almost suicidal attack missions, several being shot down. Later Magisters were all-Israeli, and incorporated extensive GRP (glass-reinforced plastics) secondary structure. About 50 were completed in Israel and many more were acquired from France and Germany to maintain strength at about 80 during the past decade. Since 1980 the Magisters have begun to be remanufactured to extend useful life into the 1990s. Some 300 engineering changes improve systems reliability, facilitate maintenance and improve cockpit displays and human engineering. The first updated aircraft was delivered in 1981.

Above and below: The Magister is still flown by the Chel Ha'Avir national aerobatic team. Their aircraft have special livery and team badge.

Sikorsky S-55

S-55 to H-19D standard

Origin: Sikorsky Aircraft Division of United Aircraft, Bridgeport, Connecticut.
Type: Utility transport helicopter.
Engine: One 800hp Wright R-1300-3 seven-cylinder radial.
Dimensions: Diameter of main rotor 53ft 0in (16·15m); length (ignoring rotors) 42ft 3in (12·88m); height 13ft 4in (4·06m); disc area 2,206sq ft (204.94m²).
Weights: Empty 5,340lb (2422kg); maximum 7,900lb (3583kg).
Performance: Maximum speed 112mph (180km/h); cruising speed 91mph (146·5km/h); ceiling (hover in ground effect) 8,600ft (2620m); range 360 miles (579km).
Armament: None.
History: First flight (S-55) November 1949, (H-19D) 1952.

The Chel Ha'Avir was singularly slow to buy a helicopter. Not until after the Suez campaign was a decision taken to build up a force of helicopters for troop carrying and resupply into front-line areas. The choice fell on the S-55, well-proven in Korea and not too ambitious for the technically over-strained Israeli force. Six were obtained, approximately equivalent to the US Army H-19D (later UH-19D) but with sand filters, different radio and other small changes (some effected locally). This series had the more powerful Wright engine, larger main rotor and down-sloping tail boom with fin-type mast carrying a smaller tail rotor, and was much superior to the earlier Wasp-powered versions. Nevertheless in Israel the very high ambient temperatures caused a severe reduction in engine power and helicopter performance. The S-55s were therefore assigned to air/sea rescue and coastal patrol where operations were generally in cooler sea-level air of higher density than in inland desert regions. At least one S-55 was occasionally seen inland but this type was not judged a success by the Chel Ha'Avir and the last were withdrawn in the mid-1960s.

Above: Three-view of H-19D series improved S-55.

Below: At least one example was obtained of the earlier S-55 series with horizontal tail boom with canted ventral fins.

Dassault Super Mystère

SMB.2

Origin: Avions Marcel Dassault, Paris.
Type: Fighter/bomber.
Engine: (As built) one SNECMA Atar 101G-3 turbojet rated at 7,440lb (3375kg) dry and 9,833lb (4460kg) with afterburner; (rebuilt) one 9,300lb 4218kg) Pratt & Whitney J52-P-8A unaugmented turbojet.
Dimensions: Span 34ft 6in (10·52m); length 46ft 4¼in (14·13m); height 14ft 11¼in (4·55m); wing area 376·7sq ft (35·0m²).
Weights: (as built) Empty 15,282lb (6932kg); loaded 19,841lb (9000kg); max 22,046lb (10,000kg); (rebuilt) empty 14,903lb (6760kg); loaded unchanged.
Performance: Maximum speed 645mph (1038km/h) at sea level, 739mph (1189km/h) at 12km; service ceiling 55,775ft (17km); range (12km, clean) 540 miles (870km).
Armament: Two 30mm DEFA 552 guns; underwing pylons for up to 2,205lb (1t) of bombs, rockets or other stores including two AIM-9 Sidewinder AAMs; internal box in belly for 35 SNEB rockets of 68mm (2·677in) calibre.
History: First flight March 1955, (production aircraft) February 1957.

Last of the series of Dassault fighters of classical tailed configuration, other than the Mirage F1 and Super Etendard, the SMB.2 resulted from a long series of progressive improvements which in this type gave supersonic speed in level flight (for the first time in a Western European fighter). No major parts were common to the Mystère IVA, and the SMB.2 was in some

Below: One of the Pratt & Whitney engined SMB.2s with the deliberately extended jetpipe to give some protection against AAMs.

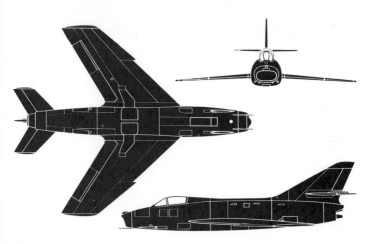

Above: Three-view of SMB.2 with original Atar engine and no tanks.

respects similar in technology and appearance to the NAA F-100, though it was smaller and much less powerful. It was an almost obvious successor to the Mystère IVA as the leading air-combat and ground attack aircraft of the Chel Ha'Avir; indeed there were few other choices. Partly on grounds of cost, an order was delayed until late 1958, when a direct contract with Dassault for 24 was concluded in Paris. They were almost all completed after the end of the Armée de l'Air order for 180, but even so all were in service by the end of 1959. A further 12 ex-Armée de l'Air SMB.2s were purchased in 1963.

Few purchases of military aircraft have been so cost effective. From the start the SMB.2 proved adequate in all respects, and though it called for

improvements in runway length and strength it was popular with pilots, and in some respects better to service than the much simpler subsonic Dassault fighters. On paper outclassed by the much faster and more agile MiG-21, it proved in practice to be at least the equal of the Russian-supplied Mach 2 aircraft and 5 June 1967 is claimed to have won 2–0 over Syrian MiG-21s. A roughly similar ratio resulted throughout the Six-Day War, eight SMB.2s being shot down and others damaged. By this time the Mirage had completely supplanted the earlier machine as the main air-combat type, and Super Mystères were put increasingly on to ground attack missions. By this time the task of keeping them on the top line was accentuated by airframe tiredness caused by prolonged rough air at low levels, and the

Above: An SMB.2 with tanks and bombs, parked, as are most Chel Ha'Avir aircraft, without any form of revetment or shelter.

Above: Profile of SMB.2 No 70, which is also seen in the photograph above. The date of this picture can be given as 1972. This three-colour camouflage scheme had been introduced a year earlier.

French embargo on supplies progressively reduced serviceability. IAI and Bet-Shemesh did their best to manufacture urgently needed parts, but the engine posed serious problems. Moreover it was becoming obsolescent in design, and in attack missions its extremely high fuel consumption resulted in very poor range and endurance. In a bold but wholly successful move the Chel Ha'Avir and IAI rebuilt the fuselage to take the Pratt & Whitney un-augmented engine used in the A-4H. This engine was lighter than the Atar and so had to be mounted further back, necessitating substantial redesign, but it cut fuel burn on combat missions by 50 to 120 per cent. A total of 26 aircraft were re-engined in 1969–73, 22 flying attack missions in the Yom Kippur War. In 1976 the 12 surviving aircraft were sold to Honduras.

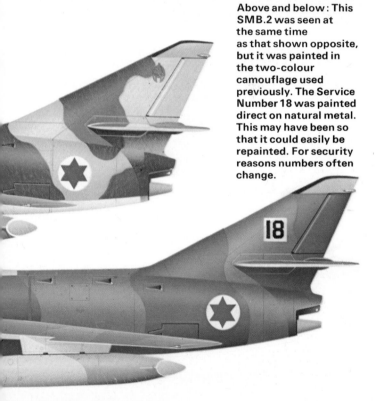

Above and below: This SMB.2 was seen at the same time as that shown opposite, but it was painted in the two-colour camouflage used previously. The Service Number 18 was painted direct on natural metal. This may have been so that it could easily be repainted. For security reasons numbers often change.

Boeing Stratocruiser
B-377M, C-97G rebuilds

Origin: Boeing Airplane Company, Seattle; rebuilt by Israel Aircraft Industries, Lod.
Type: Heavy airlift transport, inflight refuelling tanker and ECM platform.
Engines: Four 3,500hp Pratt & Whitney R-4360-59 Wasp Major 28-cylinder radials.
Dimensions: Span 141ft 3in (43·05m); length (excluding ECM) 110ft 4in (33·63m); height 38ft 3in (11·66m); wing area 1,769sq ft (164·3m²).
Weights: Empty (original) 82,500lb (37,422kg); maximum loaded 175,000 (79,380kg).
Performance: Maximum speed (new) 375mph (603km/h); cruising speed (typical) 248mph (400km/h); service ceiling (new) 30,000ft (9144m); range (max) 4,300 miles (6920km).
Armament: None.
History: First flight (XC-97) November 1944, (G) 1953.

Derived from the B-29 during World War 2, the C-97 proved one of Boeing's biggest programmes, and when the last was rolled out in July 1956 it was the 888th, of which 592 were of the final KC-97G tanker/transport for the USAF. In addition 56 commercial Model 377 Stratocruisers were sold, these

Above: Israeli military transports usually combine Chel Ha'Avir insignia with civil registration, in this case 4X-FPS. A former KC-97G, it is shown refuelling two A-4E Skyhawks. No information is available on the source of the windmill-powered hosereel units.

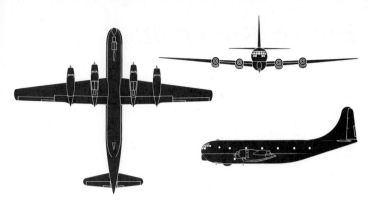

Above: Three-view of KC-97 without boom operator station.

being passenger aircraft without the strong freight floors, large rear clamshell doors and cargo-handling systems of the C-97 models. From 1956 onwards the Chel Ha'Avir recognised its need for a large cargo aircraft able to carry loads such as major armoured vehicles, bulky radars and large trucks which were beyond the capacity of the Noratlas; it also wanted an air-refuelling tanker. The obvious choice was the C-130, but the US government refused to sanction a purchase and in any case the price tag was considerably more

Above: A rare formation fly-past by three of the Chel Ha'Avir fleet in the 1960s. So far as is known, all the B-377 variants carried the same tail badge. 4X-FPY is nearest.

Left: Another Stratocruiser, 4X-FPX, which originally served as a KC-97 with the USAF.

Above: Aircraft FPY was one of the former civil Stratocruisers, with passenger windows and completely different avionics.

than $3 million — roughly five times the price of any previous Israeli aircraft. Nothing was done beyond paper studies until 1960, when a chance happening sparked off a solution. IAI had been building up its contract maintenance, overhaul and rebuild business, and among numerous civil transports at Lod were two civil Stratocruisers. The owner went bankrupt, leaving IAI with two large and unsaleable aircraft. IAI's director, the visionary Al Schwimmer, proposed not only to complete the two aircraft for the Chel Ha'Avir but to rebuild other ex-airline Stratocruisers — not subject to embargo — as military transports as good as a KC-97G.

The Chel Ha'Avir, and especially its leader Ezer Weizman, were averse to the idea. They were tired of modified junk and wanted a modern purpose-built airlifter. But finance and embargoes made that a pipe-dream, and eventually the Chel Ha'Avir gave way, with an ill grace and a long list of major modifications. IAI trimmed out the more impossible demands, such as turboprop power and rocket-assisted takeoff, but went ahead and with extreme difficulty managed to fly ten ex-PanAm Stratocruisers from Arizona to Lod where they were gutted and rebuilt in 1961–67. Many were fitted with rear fuselage and tails from C-97s, complete with large clamshell doors for vehicles and heavy freight. Strong cargo floors and mechanized handling systems were installed, together with a very capable system for heavy airdrops. Around the walls were fitted 96 troop seats, all the systems and engines were stripped and rebuilt, and most remarkable of all was a locally designed swing-tail modification based on that of the CL-44D-4 which was incorporated in two aircraft for special outsize loads.

Five were operated round the clock during the 1967 Six-Day War. In 1968 two were fitted with Flight Refuelling hosereel pods under the outer wings,

Below: This former KC-97G has numerous IAI-introduced features including a row of EW installations along the fuselage belly.

and at about this time several ex-USAF KC-97s were at last acquired to bring the total fleet up to about 15, some of which by this time were used for spares. In 1972 the Chel Ha'Avir Stratocruiser unit at Lod had three basic freighters, three swing-tail freighters, two pod-equipped tankers and two completely rebuilt for EW (electronic-warfare) roles including a powerful ECM jamming capability. One EW aircraft was shot down over Israel by an Egyptian SAM on 16 September 1971. They were all phased out of service by the end of the 1970s.

Bell 47

Model 47G and AB 47G-2

Origin: Giovanni Agusta SpA, Gallarate, Italy, under licence from Bell Helicopter, Fort Worth.
Type: Helicopter trainer and liaison.
Engine: One 260hp Lycoming VO-435-A1F or 270hp TVO-435-B1A six-cylinder opposed.
Dimensions: Diameter of main rotor 37ft 1½in (11·32m); length (ignoring rotors) 32ft 6in (9·9m); height 9ft 3in (2.82m); main-rotor disc area 1,083sq ft (100·61m²).
Weights: Empty 1,713lb (777kg); loaded 2,850lb (1293kg).
Performance: Maximum speed 105mph (169km/h); cruising speed 83mph (133km/h); service ceiling (TVO engine) 17,600ft (5365m); range 250 miles (402km).
Armament: None.
History: First flight (47) December 1945, (AB 47G) May 1954.

One of the most widely used helicopters in history, the Bell 47 was utilised in large numbers in the Korean war as a casevac, liaison and training machine, and at the same time went into licence-production by Agusta in Italy which built up a wide market throughout Europe and the Middle East. In 1965 the Chel Ha'Avir acquired 15 Bell 47G and Agusta-Bell AB 47G-2 helicopters. Though able to carry a slung load of 1,000lb (454kg) they have always

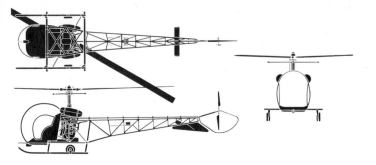

Above: Three-view of typical 47G.

served as trainers, with occasional use in the VIP liaison role, as photographic/TV vehicles and in general utility tasks. They were all withdrawn from service in 1970–71 and sold outside Israel.

Below: The Chel Ha'Avir bought a mixed bag of Bell and Agusta-built machines and used them for six years. None was ever seen in an armed or casevac role, and most were used (as in this fine picture) as helicopter pilot trainers at the Chel Ha'Avir school at Hatzerim. Today there is no low-cost trainer in use.

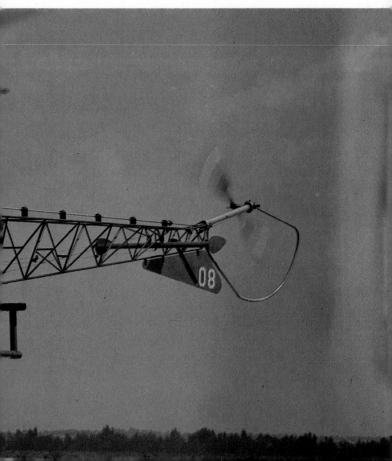

SE Alouette II
SE 313B, SA 318C

Origin: Sud-Aviation (later Aérospatiale), Paris.
Type: Light utility helicopter.
Engine: One 400hp Turboméca Artouste IIC turboshaft derated to flat rating of 360hp maintained under hot/high conditions; (318C) one 530hp Turboméca Astazou IIA derated to 360hp.
Dimensions: Diameter of main rotor 33ft 5½in (10·2m); length (excl main rotor) 31ft 11¾in (9·75m); height 9ft 0in (2·75m); main-rotor disc area 879·5sq ft (81·7m²).
Weights: Empty 1,973lb (895kg); loaded 3,527lb (1600kg).
Performance: Maximum speed 115mph (185km/h); cruising speed 102mph (165km/h); service ceiling 7,050ft (2150m); range (max fuel) 350 miles (565km), (max payload) 62 miles (100km).
Armament: Not fitted.
History: First flight (313B) 12 March 1955.

Thanks to pioneering development by the Société Turboméca, led by Joseph Szydlowski, France led the world in applying gas-turbine propulsion in jet, turboprop and turboshaft forms to all kinds of light aircraft. Nowhere were the advantages more immediately manifest than in the field of helicopters, where the SNCASE 3130 (later redesignated SE 313B) brought a quantum jump in flight performance, payload and reliability, apart from a switch to less-volatile turbine fuel. Broadly similar to a Bell 47, but more capable in seating a pilot and four passengers or carrying a cargo load of 1,322lb (600kg), the Alouette II sold readily and eventually notched up a tally of 1,300 to 126 military and civil customers in 46 countries. Israel was a relatively early buyer, opening negotiations in 1956. Ultimately an evaluation quantity of five was delivered in 1957–58, at which time the S-55 was the only other helicopter in Chel Ha'Avir service. A total of 15 Alouette IIs were acquired from 1957 to 1969, the later acquisitions being Astazou-powered SA 318Cs. Two Alouette IIs remain in the Chel Ha'Avir inventory for VIP transport.

Right: An SE 313B on a liaison mission. Reports that the Chel Ha'Avir also used Alouette III helicopters are unfounded.

Below: An Alouette II in typical up-country surroundings. The engine is flat-rated not to lose power in hot/high conditions.

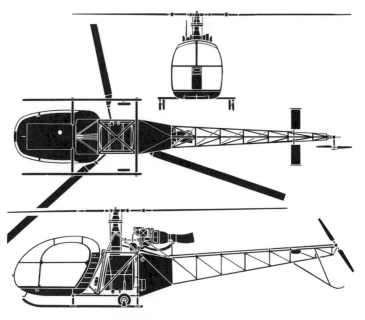

Above: Three-view of SE 313B Alouette II.

Consolidated-Vultee Valiant

BT-13A

Origin: Convair, Vultee Field Division, Downey, California.

Today almost forgotten, the Vultee Valiant was one of the two basic trainers of the USAAF in World War 2, the BT-13A with the 450hp P & W R-985-AN-1 Wasp Junior being the most common variant, and it was also mass-produced as the SNV family for the Navy. A stressed-skin fixed-gear machine with large 'glasshouse' canopy over tandem seats, it was produced at Downey at such a rate that P & W's engine output could not keep pace and 1,693 had the Wright Whirlwind. On one day alone 123 were flown off the line, and total deliveries were 11,537. Of these two were acquired in the USA in late 1948 and brought to Israel by surface means, arriving in early 1949. They probably served as pilot trainers; they could have carried machine guns or bombs but probably did not have to do so. Maximum speed was 180mph (290km/h) and endurance six hours at 120mph (193km/h).

Above: Front and side elevations of standard BT-13A Valiant.

Miles Gemini

M.65

Origin: Miles Aircraft, Woodley, Reading.

The M.65 Gemini was one of the few really successful British lightplanes of the post-war era. Though made of wood it was tough, long-lasting and extremely attractive, and features included a four-seat cabin with vertically hinged side doors, a giant one-piece blown windscreen, patented Miles "double-wing" high-lift flaps and neat main landing gears with levered suspension for rough fields and small Miles electric actuators to retract them backwards into the nacelles. There were several sub-types, G-AKEP being one of the common Gemini 1A models with two 100hp Blackburn Cirrus Minor 2 engines, giving a cruising speed of 135mph (217km/h). It was bought in Britain and arrived in the infant state of Israel in May 1948, immediately joining the Chel Ha'Avir.

Below: The Gemini 1A photographed after arrival in Israel.

Piaggio P.149

P.149D

Origin: Piaggio & C SpA, licence-built by Focke-Wulf and Blume.

One of the most attractive military trainers of the post-war era, the P.149 combined stressed-skin construction, a four- or five-seat cabin with giant blown sliding canopy, retractable tricycle landing gear and a reliable American engine driving a Piaggio constant-speed three-blade propeller. It flew in 1953 but did not enter production until chosen for the reborn Federal German Luftwaffe, 88 being supplied from Italy and 177 being made in Germany. Three found their way to the Chel Ha'Avir from Uganda in 1968 and served until 1972. It has proved impossible to establish their role which could have been aerobatic pilot training or just utility transport for senior officers.

Above: Front and side elevations of Piaggio P.149D.

Hiller 360

Model 360, UH-12B

Origin: Hiller Helicopters, Palo Alto, California.

The Hiller 360 was the only helicopter to offer competition to the Bell 47 as the standard light utility machine for military and civil use in the period 1946–55. The original 360 had a 178hp Franklin engine and seated three abreast on a bench at the front. By 1951 the design had been refined into the UH-12B with a 200hp Franklin 6V4 engine and conventional pilot controls replacing the overhead stick leading direct to the rotor hub. Most UH-12Bs were two-seat trainers for the US forces, though some carried two litter casualties externally. The Chel Ha'Avir obtained the prototype 360 and a UH-12B in May 1951, and used them as its first utility and training helicopters.

Below: The Hiller UH-12B: the 360 was generally similar.

Dassault Mirage III

IIICJ, RJ and BJ

Origin: Avions Marcel Dassault, Paris.
Type: (CJ) day fighter/bomber, (RJ) fighter reconnaissance, (BJ) trainer with attack capability.
Engine: One SNECMA Atar 9B3 augmented turbojet rated at 9,370lb (4250kg) dry and 13,228lb (6000kg) with maximum afterburner, replaced around 1970 by Atar 9C rated at 14,110lb (6400kg).
Dimensions: Span (all) 26ft 11½in (8·22m); length (C) 48ft 4in (14·73m), (R) 50ft 10¼in (15·5m), (B) 50ft 6¼in (15·4m); height 13ft 11½in (4·25m); wing area 375·13sq ft (34·85m²).
Weights: Empty (C) 13,570lb (6156kg), (R) 14,020lb (6359kg), (B) 13,820lb (6270kg); loaded (C, clean) 19,700lb (8936kg), (R, B, max) 26,455lb (12,000kg).
Performance: Maximum speed (clean) 863mph (1390km/h) at sea level, 1,386mph (2230km/h, Mach 2·1) above 30,000ft (9144m); service ceiling (Mach 1·8) 55,775ft (17km), normal subsonic ceiling, 41,000ft (12·5km); range (two tanks, high altitude) 820 miles (1320km); tactical radius (no external fuel) 180 miles (290km).
Armament: (C, R) two 30mm DEFA 5—52 guns with 125 rounds each, plus two AIM-9 Sidewinder or Shafrir (originally also one Matra R.511) AAMs, or two bombs or other stores of up to 1,000lb (454kg) each; (B) as above but without guns.
History: First flight (Mirage III) November 1956, (production IIIC) October 1960.

By chance this trim tailless delta, originally planned as a pure interceptor for the Armée de l'Air, matured at precisely the time the USAF had set its sights on an enormous swing-wing multi-role aircraft (TFX) and Britain had given up fighters altogether, so it had the field virtually to itself. In any case Dassault was the obvious company to turn to when it was clear that such Arab air-combat aircraft as the MiG-21 made the acquisition of new fighters a matter of top priority. It is a matter of historical fact that once the British FD.2 had gained a world speed record 300mph (483km/h) faster than the previous best, Marcel Dassault himself was totally sold on the tailless delta configuration, but larger than his existing Mirage I and matched to the power of a new family of Atar engines being developed by SNECMA. This made the Mirage III almost the only choice open to the Chel Ha'Avir, but its purchase was for the first time a matter of some technical risk. Never before had Israel been in the position of buying a new aircraft, and this time it was to be the most costly purchase to date, and one on which the future existence of Israel would clearly depend.

Above and right: Two Mirage IIICJ fighters in their original unpainted state, with no external load except tanks. Israel showed great wisdom in selecting guns (in 1960 widely considered to be obsolete) instead of the optional booster rocket unit.

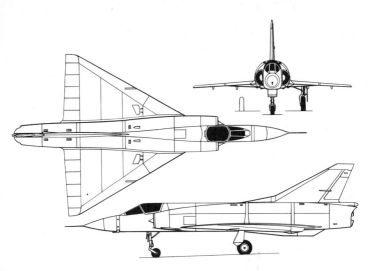

Above: Three-view of Mirage IIICJ as originally delivered.

Above: Probably taken in 1971, this photograph depicts a Mirage IIICJ still unpainted at a time when almost all other Chel Ha'Avir combat aircraft were camouflaged. Tanks are 137gal (623-lit).

Gen Ezer Weizman insisted on the closest collaboration with the French, and on a thorough technical evaluation. Col Danny Shapira was permitted to fly the Mirage III-001 in early 1959, long before any other foreign pilot, and he was soon an enthusiastic convert; indeed at several points his testing was ahead in timing of Glavany and the other company and Armée de l'Air pilots. Many modifications resulted from his recommendations. At the same time politics delayed signature of a contract until 1961, when the final purchase totalled 72 fighters (designated IIICJ, J for Juif being typical humour of Bernard Wacquet, Dassault sales director) plus four IIIB trainers. The Chel Ha'Avir chose to fit guns, and thus did not have the booster rocket which in retrospect appears much less attractive than it did in 1960. Subsequently IAI greatly strengthened its electronic expertise in partnership with CSF, the parent company of the Mirage's Cyrano 1 *bis* radar, and in the 1970s blossomed into Elta Electronics with capability to produce much better radars of its own (see Kfir). Several of the fighters were modified with recon noses as IIIRJ aircraft (shorter and less powerful than other IIIR variants which were derived from the later Mirage IIIE).

Deliveries took place in 1962–64 and about 65 were combat-ready at the start of the Six-Day War in June 1967. This war in fact was to a small

Above: Mirage IIICJ.

degree precipitated by the decision of the French President, Gen de Gaulle, to espouse the Arab cause and place an embargo on all sales to Israel, thus cutting off even the Mirage spare parts. In that war the combat performance of the Mirage was not only brilliant, being skilfully flown in attack and air-combat on as many as eight sorties per aircraft per day, but it was instantly seen in newspapers and on TV screens all over the world. Though marginally inferior to the MiG-21F in manoeuvrability, and almost outclassed by later MiG-21 versions, the Mirage shot down some 48 Arab aircraft in that war for the loss of a single machine (in lone combat with eight MiGs). Six other Mirages were lost to ground fire. Subsequently IAI, Bet-Shemesh, Elta and other companies replaced France as the source of hardware support, and in fact have progressively updated the Mirages with better systems and electronics. Today the remaining Mirages still equip one squadron.

Below: Today the surviving Mirage IIICJs look like this. Apart from the new camouflage scheme the most striking difference is the improved multi-flap nozzle of the Atar 9C engine fitted in the 1970s. The avionic fit has also undergone progressive changes, and IAI has done much to prolong the safe life of the structure. Stencils are in Hebrew.

Pilatus Turbo-Porter

PC-6/A1-H2

Origin: Pilatus Flugzeugwerke, Stans, Switzerland.
Type: STOL utility transport.
Engine: One 573hp Turboméca Astazou XII turboprop.
Dimensions: Span 49ft 8in (15·13m); length 36ft 4½in (11·08m); height 10ft 6in (3·2m); wing area 310sq ft (28·8m²).
Weights: Empty 2,623lb (1190kg); loaded 4,850lb (2200kg).
Performance: Maximum speed 174mph (280km/h); cruising speed 135mph (217km/h); service ceiling 32,000ft (9750m); range (max internal fuel) 790 miles (1270km).
History: First flight (PC-6) May 1959, (A1-H2) May 1961.

A natural successor to the old Norseman, the Swiss Porter is a functional and angular utility transport with outstanding STOL performance. Originally fitted with the same piston engine as the Do 27 (though it is a larger aircraft, with up to ten passengers in the unobstructed main cabin) it was developed by 1961 with the first of a series of turboprop engines which offered even better performance. The prototype of the turboprop A1 model so impressed the Israeli Ministry of Defence in 1963 that the actual aircraft was bought on the spot. In 1968 it was joined by a second example with the French Astazou

Dornier Do 27

Do 27Q

Origin: Dornier GmbH, Friedrichshafen/Bodensee.
Type: STOL transport, ambulance, observation, survey and rescue.
Engine: One 274hp Lycoming GSO-480-B1A6 six-cylinder opposed.
Dimensions: Span 39ft 4½in (12·0m); length 32ft 5¾in (9·9m); height 9ft 2¼in (2·8m); wing area 208·8sq ft (19·4m²).
Weights: Empty 2,568lb (1165kg); loaded 4,078lb (1850kg).
Performance: Maximum speed 155mph (250km/h); cruising speed 135mph (217km/h); service ceiling 22,310ft (6800m); range 845 miles (1360km).
History: First flight June 1955, (H-2) November 1958.

Below: Three-view of Dornier Do 27Q (small tyres).

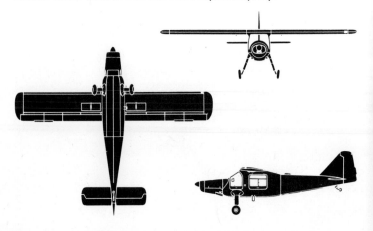

Above: The prototype Pilatus PC-6/A1 Turbo-Porter soon after its purchase. All four chocks are neatly chained together.

engine. In the Chel Ha'Avir they have served chiefly as ambulance and cargo machines, able to carry about 1,650lb (750kg) of payload including items up to 16ft 5in (5m) in length. The floor hatch permits smaller items to be air-dropped. The aircraft has also been used for paratroops, though this is not a routine duty.

After World War 2 Dornier managed to reassemble a design team at Seville, Spain, where the prototype of an extremely advanced and attractive STOL (short takeoff and landing) light transport, the Do 25, flew in June 1954. With a more powerful (274hp) engine and six seats instead of four this became the Do 27, which sold well in many markets, including 428 for the Bundeswehr. In 1964 Israel bought the Do 27Q, in which the same Lycoming engine, driving a Hartzell three-blade propeller, enabled loads of 1,500lb (680kg) to be carried with improved flight performance. At full load, in temperate conditions, a height of 50ft (15m) could be reached 722ft (220m) from a standing start; landing from the same height took only 590ft (180m). The Chel Ha'Avir bought about 35 of this model, which have since served with conspicuous success in countless utilitarian roles in the harshest and hottest environments.

Below: The Do 27 was one of the relatively few types which proved fully able to cope with the harsh Chel Ha'Avir environment. Note the oversize tyres for use on rough surfaces and soft sand.

Sikorsky S-58

S-58B, CH-34A

Origin: Sikorsky Aircraft Division of United Aircraft Corporation, Stratford, Connecticut.
Type: Multi-role transport helicopter.
Engine: One 1,525hp Wright R-1820-84B Cyclone nine-cylinder radial.
Dimensions: Diameter of main rotor 56ft 0in (17·07m); length (ignoring rotors) 46ft 9 in (14·25m); height 15ft 11in (4·85m); main-rotor disc area 2,460sq ft (228·54m²).
Weights: Empty 7,900lb (3583kg); loaded 13,000lb (5897kg).
Performance: Maximum speed 122mph (196km/h); cruising speed 97mph (156km/h); service ceiling 9,100ft (2774m); range (max fuel with 10 per cent reserve) 248 miles (400km).
Armament: Usually none, but various guns and rocket launchers occasionally fitted for front-line duties.
History: First flight (S-58) March 1954.

The S-58 was the first really capable helicopter used by the Chel Ha'Avir. So far as is known, no approach was made to Westland in Britain, whose licensed version with turbine engines offered much greater payload and performance, and the basic S-58 with a single piston engine (the same engine in many respects as that of the old B-17s) was found to be adequate for the operational needs. Seven aircraft of essentially S-58B type were purchased as civil machines from Sikorsky in 1958. A year later 24 CH-34A military helicopters were passed on to Israel by the German Navy, these were fitted with additional avionic equipment, and were further distinguished by the exhaust on the left side instead of under the nose. Until 1966 the S-58 was used intensively as the only available vehicle for front-line resupply, casevac from the battlefield, Commando attack, anti-terrorist and close-support duties, carrying every conceivable kind of load up to a ton in weight. Light aircraft, Jeeps and similar loads were often carried as slung cargo, while internal loads included virtually all the fuel and ammunition needed by front-line forces. Pilots were instructed in ways of evading fighters, and some S-58s were fitted with local pilot and engine armour, various armament fits and special avionics including ADF and ILS. Normal loads could include 18 troops or eight litters (stretchers). These helicopters were progressively withdrawn in the early 1970s.

Below: Profile illustration of the same machine as shown in the photograph. It is an ex-German Marineflieger CH-34A with numerous differences compared with the machines bought new.

Above: Three-view of typical basic S-58 (original engine).

Above: This fine photograph shows one of the CH-34C utility transport helicopters bought secondhand from Federal Germany in 1960. Throughout the 1960s the S-58 was the most important transport helicopter in the Chel Ha'Avir, though the first Super Frelons arrived in time for the Six-Day War. It is remarkable that IAI was not asked to update them with the PT6T coupled turbine engines.

Aérospatiale Super Frelon

SA 321 K

Origin: Sud-Aviation (later Aérospatiale), Paris.
Type: Transport and assault helicopter.
Engines: (As built) three 1,550hp Turboméca Turmo IIIC6 turboshafts, (as modified) three 1,870hp General Electric T58-GE-16 turboshafts.
Dimensions: Diameter of main rotor 62ft 0in (18·9m); length (ignoring rotors) 63ft 7¾in (19·4m); height 21ft 10¼in (6·66m); main-rotor disc area 3,020sq ft (280·55m²).
Weights: Empty (with floats) 15,055lb (6829kg), (without) 14,420lb (6541kg); loaded 28,660lb (13,000kg).
Performance: Maximum speed 171mph (275km/h); cruising speed 155mph (250km/h); service ceiling 10,335ft (3150m); range 509 miles (820km).
Armament: Not usually fitted.
History: First flight December 1962, (production type) November 1965.

Last of the French types to be procured for the Chel Ha'Avir, the three-engined Super Frelon was designed by Sud-Aviation with technical assistance from Sikorsky, and with the main gearbox and transmission produced by Fiat (now Aeritalia). The initial 321G model was an amphibious anti-submarine search/attack helicopter for the French Aéronavale. When this was being developed, Israel opened negotiations for the purchase of 24 of a multi-role overland assault and airlift transport model designated 321K.

Below: Complete designations for Chel Ha'Avir Super Frelons have not been published; this is an amphibious example, No 09.

Below: In contrast, Super Frelon No 08 is non-amphibious, seen here with rotors turning on a Chel Ha'Avir desert airfield.

Above: Three-view of the non-amphibious SA 321 version.

Below: A recent photograph of air/sea rescue training using amphibious SA 321 K No 408. The censor has obliterated unit badges at nose and tail, but it is still possible to see several avionics aerials which were not fitted at the time of delivery from France.

Eventually a contract was signed in 1965 for twelve, the first six having amphibious capability and the next six (and the planned second batch of 12) having the large stabilizing floats removed. All have an unobstructed main cabin roughly 6ft (about 2m) in width and height, with a full-section rear ramp/door for loading heavy cargo or vehicles. Seating can be provided for 30 troops, and in Chel Ha'Avir service the normal cargo limit is 9,921lb (4500kg), though the brochure figure is 11,023lb (5000kg). The same weight can be lifted as an external slung load.

In the event, six (with floats) were delivered by the Six-Day War in 1967, and three of the remainder. Then the French government embargoed further deliveries, previously paid for, but allowed the remaining three to be delivered after the war. The 12 delivered accomplished more in their first decade than any other 12 military helicopters in history. They flew day and night in the Six-Day War, often putting down ground forces behind enemy battlefields and in particular enabling the Golan Heights to be taken. They flew Commandos deep into Middle Egypt to attack the Quena Dam and Nag Hammadi power station on the Upper Nile, and on 28 December 1968 flew another Commando force to attack MEA aircraft at Beirut Airport in retaliation for raids from the Lebanon into northern Israel. The eight survivors have been much modified and will continue into the 1990s.

Below: Super Frelon No 09 pictured arriving at a desert airbase. The dark lump above the nose is a winch, not fitted to the non-amphibious machine pictured opposite. Engines are now GE T58s.

Above: Another recent shot of a Super Frelon in active service, in this case with all insignia except the Israeli national emblem obliterated. Removing the floats does not affect payload.

Beechcraft Queen Air

B80, RU-21

Origin: Beech Aircraft, Wichita, Kansas.
Type: Liaison, utility and trainer.
Engines: Two 380hp Lycoming IGSO-540-A1D six-cylinder opposed.
Dimensions: Span 50ft 3in (15·32m); length 35ft 6in (10·82m); height 14ft 2½in (4·33m); wing area 277sq ft (25·73m²).
Weights: Empty 5,040lb (2286kg); loaded 8,800lb (3992kg).
Performance: Maximum speed 248mph (400km/h); cruising speed 183mph (294km/h); service ceiling 26,800ft (8168m); range (max fuel, with allowances) 1,560 miles (2510km).
History: First flight (Queen Air) August 1958, (Model 80) June 1961.

Like most Beechcraft the Queen Air was from the start an up-market twin with all-metal structure, comprehensive systems and avionics and luxurious furnishing. Though overtaken at the top end of the company range by various King Air turboprops the Queen Air remains the top of the piston-engined products. The first for the Chel Ha'Avir were bought in 1974, and subsequent purchases took the total to 12. All have two-pilot flight decks, and several are used full-time in the multi-engine pilot training role, preparing pilots for the C-130 and other large fixed-wing aircraft. The main cabin can seat up to nine, and at least two of the Queen Airs are VIP aircraft with the optional air-conditioning system and special furnishing. Most are used for general liaison, with the overriding task of flying all local

---

Dornier Do 28

Do 28B-1

Origin: Dornier GmbH, Friedrichshafen.
Type: Light STOL utility transport.
Engines: Two 290hp Lycoming IO-540-A six-cylinder opposed.
Dimensions: Span 45ft 3½in (13·8m); length 29ft 6in (9·00m); height 9ft 2in (2·8m); wing area (excluding stub wings) 241sq ft (22·4m²).
Weights: Empty 3,960lb (1800kg); loaded 6,000lb (2722kg).
Performance: Maximum speed 184mph (290km/h); cruising speed 150mph (242km/h); service ceiling 19,400ft (5900m); range (max payload, no reserve) 768 miles (1235km).
History: First flight (Do 28) 29 April 1959, (28B-1) April 1963.

Almost a twin-engined version of the extremely successful Do 27, the Do 28 was a simple way of fitting more power, the two engines being attached to the ends of a short stub wing projecting on each side of the nose beneath the cockpit. The spatted main gears are cantilevered beneath the engines, and other features include fuel in wing tanks (overwing fuelling), fixed leading-edge slots, double-slotted flaps and provision for pneumatic de-icer boots. The cockpit, with the same breathtaking glass area as on the Do 27, seats a pilot and passenger, and in the passenger role the main cabin has six passengers facing each other on triple transverse bench seats. The first Do 28B-1 was supplied in 1971 and a number (reported unofficially to be ten) are today being used very successfully, the takeoff and landing distances being better than any other Chel Ha'Avir fixed-wing machines. The type is available with special role equipment (eg, for photography and casevac) but is usually employed carrying cargo and personnel on such duties as anti-terrorist patrol.

Persistent reports that the much larger Do 28D Skyservant is used by the

Above: The Chel Ha'Avir insists its Queen Airs are commercially bought B80s, and denies the report that it uses ex-US Army RU-21 electronic surveillance aircraft to monitor activity over the border.

commanders to battle stations within hours in the event of mobilization.

Since 1975 several ex-US Army RU-21 electronic surveillance aircraft are said to have been acquired in a direct government transfer. Basically of B80 standard, they are claimed to monitor activity around Israel's borders and especially in the Sinai.

Chel Ha'Avir are without foundation. It is true that the Skyservant was evaluated, but no order was subsequently placed by the Chel Ha'Avir. Although no announcement had been made at the time this book went to press, in mid-1982, it is likely that the Chel Ha'Avir will purchase the Do 228 to supplement or replace the earlier Dorniers at present in service.

Below: Like the Do 27Q the Do 28B proved very successful. This model has an enlarged tailplane and fuel in the wingtips.

McDonnell Douglas A-4 Skyhawk

A-4H, TA-4H, A-4E, TA-4J, A-4N (in that order)

Origin: Douglas Aircraft Co, Long Beach, California.

Type: Single-seat attack, (TA) two-seat pilot trainer.

Engine: One Pratt & Whitney J52 unaugmented turbojet, (E, J) 8,300lb (3765kg) J52-P-6 or 6A, (H, and F/J re-engined) 9,300lb (4218kg) J52-P-8A, (N, and F/H re-engined) 11,200lb (5080kg) J52-P-408A.

Dimensions: Span 27ft 6in (8·38m); length (excluding FR probe), (E, H, short jetpipe) 40ft 3¼in (12·27m), (E, F, long pipe) 42ft 10in (13·05m), (TA, short pipe) 42ft 7¼in (12·98m), (N, long pipe) 42ft 10¾in (13·075m); height (single-seat) 15ft 0in (4·57m); wing area 260sq ft (24·16m²).

Weights: Empty (E) 9,853lb (4469kg), (H) 9,940lb (4509kg), (TA) 10,150lb (4604kg), (N) 10,990lb (4985kg); normal loaded (all) 24,500lb (11,113kg).

Performance: Maximum speed (clean) (E) 674mph (1085km/h), (H) 685mph (1102km/h), (TA) 654mph (1052km/h); (with 4,000lb, 1814kg bombload) (E) 620mph (998km/h), (H) 631mph (1015km/h), (N) 646mph (1040km/h); service ceiling (N, full external load) 42,250ft (12,880m); range (N, max ferry) 2,350 miles (3780km); combat radius (N) 385 miles (620km).

Armament: All single-seaters now equipped with two 30mm DEFA 552A guns each with 150 rounds; normal maximum external load 8,200lb (3720kg) though N can be loaded to pylon limits of (centreline) 3,500lb

Above: 30mm ammunition shows that even the original A-4H model was upgraded with the hard-hitting DEFA gun, now on all versions.

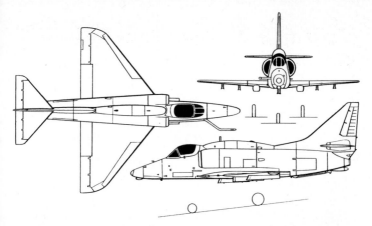

Above: Three-view of A-4N Skyhawk II prior to fitting long jetpipe.

(1588kg), (inners) 2,250lb (1020kg) and (outers) 1,000lb (454kg). Extremely wide range of stores, plus Shafrir for self-protection.
History: First flight June 1954, (H) October 1967, (N) June 1972.

Famed for meeting a 1952 US Navy requirement for a carrier-based attack aircraft whilst weighing just half the permitted limit, the A-4 Skyhawk proved to be so outstanding in its cost/effectiveness that, despite the emergence of later replacements, it kept being improved and updated and remained in production for a remarkable 26 years, from 1953 until 1979. Altogether 2,960 were built, 555 of these being dual-control trainers. Though the US Navy and Marine Corps were by far the largest customers,

Above: Airbrakes open, a Skyhawk (probably an A-4E) shows its flight-refuelling probe, longer jetpipe and five main weapon pylons, plus a Shafrir AAM pylon near the left wingtip. The hook is striped.

Left: An ex-US Navy A-4E, with the original round-topped fin, fitted in Israel with updated avionics including the "camel hump".

Israel came second, and, as in the case of several important combat-aircraft programmes, introduced several important modifications to increase the effectiveness and survivability of the A-4 in Chel Ha'Avir service.

Basic features of the A-4 are its extreme design elegance and simplicity. Wherever possible items were made to serve multiple functions; in fact chief engineer Ed Heinemann's philosophy was to "take the best jet engine, put a saddle for the jockey on it, put a wing under it and leave out everything else". The wing was made as a single integral tank, so small it did not need to fold. The stalky main landing gears folded forwards, the leg lying in a fairing under the wing box and the wheel rotating 90° to lie ahead of it. Powerful slats were fitted to a wing of lower thickness/chord ratio than slats had ever been fitted to before (except the YF-100) and high-frequency "buzz" over

Above: The first Skyhawks to arrive in Israel were of the A-4H type, built for the Chel Ha'Avir with 30mm guns and Rafael Mahat avionics. They have subsequently been largely remanufactured.

the rudder was cured by putting the skin down the centre of that surface and the half ribs on the outside! Above all, the A-4 carried extremely heavy offensive loads yet remained one of the most agile aircraft in the sky.

The original order for 48 A-4H and two TA-4H was placed in 1966. Broadly similar to the A-4F and TA-4F, but with a braking parachute and square-tipped fin, these aircraft were fitted with 30mm guns and equipped a combat-ready squadron before the end of 1968, one of the first of many extremely successful missions being a strike on the strongly defended El Fatah terrorist base on the east bank of the Jordan in 1968. A subsequent contract was placed for 42 A-4H and eight TA-4H, the two-seater making its first flight on 15 April 1969. While deliveries of these aircraft were in progress the US government released an initial batch of 25 ex-US Navy A-4E, and by 1974 the Chel Ha'Avir had received 60 A-4E and -F second-hand single-seaters plus 17 of the useful TA-4J simplified dual trainers. Some of these were replacements flown dismantled in C-5As to replace losses in the 1973 war.

From late 1972 the Chel Ha'Avir also received the more advanced A-4N, a special export derivative of the A-4M Skyhawk II with much-improved systems and numerous other changes including a new canopy and wind-screen giving improved pilot view. This was also the first model received by the Chel Ha'Avir with the "camel hump" filled with additional avionics. With the collaboration of US suppliers Israeli field teams retrofitted the distinctive dorsal hump to all its single-seat Skyhawks, as well as imported and locally produced ECM pods.

Not many of these changes had been effected when the Yom Kippur War broke out. In this gruelling conflict the Chel Ha'Avir Skyhawks flew as many attack missions as all other types combined. In the process the six squadrons

Below: This is how the A-4H Skyhawks look today, with "camel hump" and long jetpipe to improve protection against heat-seeking missiles. The H was one of the first models with the flat-top fin.

lost 53 aircraft in action, more than half the total (102) of all Chel Ha'Avir losses in that war. This emphatically does not imply vulnerability, indeed the Israelis have always been most enthusiastic about this aircraft, and regard it as the best attack platform available — and, until the advent of the F-16, as the most agile combat aircraft in the Middle East. There are many instances of bombed-up Skyhawks out-fighting MiG-21s, and clean aircraft have demonstrated their ability to out-turn even the MiG-17. In May 1970 an A-4H shot down two Syrian MiG-17s over Lebanon, one with its guns and the other with unguided rockets. Almost all (49) of the downed Skyhawks were hit by ground fire, probably three-quarters by the CW-homing SA-6 missile which was deadly and could not be jammed or dodged. Even so, numerous surviving Skyhawks regained base with severe battle damage, one after being hit in the wing by an AA-2 Atoll AAM.

After that war further supplies of the then-new A-4N brought up the total of that model to 129 (not 117 as usually reported), making an overall total of 279 single-seaters and 27 two-seaters. Of these sufficient remain for a sustained inventory of about 100, with plenty in reserve for attrition. The A-4Ns and some of the earlier single-seaters have been fitted with extended jetpipes to reduce the IR (infra-red) signature and explode warheads of IR-homing missiles (notably SA-7) well behind the tail. The Skyhawk is expected to remain in service until replaced by the Lavi in about 1992.

Above: The camouflage
on this A-4E includes a
green of an unusually
bright yellowish shade.
Apart from the TA-4J
this is the only variant
in the Chel Ha'Avir to
have the original round-
top fin. This variant
is one of those fitted
with "camel hump"
avionics after arriving
in Israel. Flight
refuelling probes are
carried mainly to draw
fuel from KC-130 tank-
ers or from Buddy pods
(with hosereel) such as
that carried on the
centreline pylon of the
A-4H on pages 102-3.

Left: The Chel Ha'Avir
uses both the TA-4H and
(with curved fin-top)
TA-4J, the tandem
cockpits being almost
identical. Today both
trainers have the P-8A
engine with extended
jetpipe (single seaters
having the more
powerful P-408A) and a
ribbon-type braking
parachute. Here a
pupil and instructor are
about to taxi out on a
weapons-training
sortie.

McDonnell Douglas F-4 Phantom

F-4E, RF-4E

Origin: McDonnell Aircraft Co, St Louis.
Type: Two-seater fighter and attack, (RF) multi-sensor reconnaissance.
Engines: Two General Electric J79-GE-17 augmented turbojets each rated at 11,870lb (5384kg) dry and 17,900lb (8119kg) with maximum afterburner.
Dimensions: Span 38ft 4in (11·68m); length 63ft 0in (19·2m); height 16ft 5in (5·0m); wing area 530sq ft (49·24m²).
Weights: Empty 30,328lb (13,757kg), (RF, about 31,250lb, 14,175kg); loaded (subsonic 7·75g) 58,000lb (26,309kg), (max, subsonic 5·17g) 61,795lb (28,030kg), (RF) max 57,320lb (26,000kg).
Performance: Maximum speed 1,432mph (2304km/h, Mach 2·17) at 36,000ft (10,973m); typical cruising speed 572mph (920km/h); service ceiling (clean) 58,750ft (17,907m); range (ferry, three tanks, full allowances) 1,611 miles (2593km); combat radius (four AIM-7E + 11 M117 bombs + two tanks, max wt takeoff) 306 miles (492km).
Armament: One 20mm M61A1 gun with 639 rounds (and see text); four AIM-7E-2 or related Sparrow medium-range radar-homing AAMs recessed under fuselage and two pairs of Rafael Shafrir or Sidewinder AAMs on inboard wing pylons; centreline pylon for 600US-gal (500gal, 2270 litre) tank (about 4,500lb, 2040kg) or ordnance loads to 3,020lb (1370kg); four wing pylons for additional ordnance loads totalling 12,980lb (5888kg)

Below: Substantial numbers of F-4E Phantom IIs, including this example, were in Chel Ha'Avir service by the start of the Yom Kippur War launched by Arab nations on 6 October 1973.

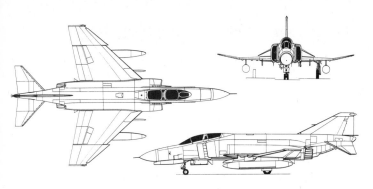

Above: Three-view of F-4E carrying tanks only.

or two 370US-gal (308gal, 1400 litre) tanks. (RF) none.
History: First flight (XF4H-1) May 1958, (F-4E) August 1965, (RF-4E)
September 1970.

Unquestionably the greatest fighter of the 1960s, and one of the greatest
combat aircraft of all time, the Phantom II was designed as a gunless all-
weather carrier-based interceptor for the US Navy and Marine Corps,
entering service as the F-4B in June 1961. In a spate of world records it hit
the headlines, and it was soon clear that it was not only an outstanding
performer but an aircraft of exceptional versatility. Evaluation by the US Air
Force in 1961 confirmed that in almost all respects the basic F-4B out-
performed all the specialist day fighter, all-weather interceptor and attack

**Below: This photo-
graph was in the
first batch released
by the Chel Ha'Avir
showing Phantoms
in Israel. It has been
seen before, but is
still one of the best
for giving an indica-
tion of what the
Israelis took on in
terms of size,
complexity and cost.**

Above: Phantom No 198 is one of the unarmed RF-4E reconnaissance platforms (which in the Chel Ha'Avir are not quite unarmed).

Below: This F-4E, No 270, was put on public display together with its M61A-1 gun and the full spectrum of stores it can carry.

aircraft of the USAF, and in March 1962 the first of many large orders was placed for a land-based USAF version, the minimum-change F-4C. The F-4D followed, more tailored to land attack missions, and the RF-4C multi-sensor reconnaissance aircraft. Vietnam experience showed the need for an internal gun and slatted wing, and these were eventually fitted to the F-4E, configured with a new solid-state radar in a longer but slimmer nose, an extra fuel tank to preserve balance at the tail, and more powerful engines to match the greater weight.

Soon after the production F-4E became available in 1967 the Chel Ha'Avir, having made a careful evaluation previously, sought permission to place an order. Though much larger than previous Israeli fighters, and at about $4·5 million by far the most costly, the sheer capability of the Phantom was proven in battle and transcended anything then in the Middle East. In particular it offered a long-range kill capability with radar-guided Sparrow AAMs that was lacking in the Chel Ha'Avir at that time. State Department

Below: Fuel streams from the vents as an F-4E, No 161 with
yellow rudder, pulls out with part-flap, slats open and hook out.

approval was granted, and in 1969 Israeli flight crews (pilots and back-
seaters, variously called observers or navigators) and specialist ground
tradesmen underwent courses in the USA, preparatory to the first delivery
in September 1969.

The initial batch numbered 50, together with six of the specially developed
RF-4E model, virtually an RF-4C with the greater power and aft-fuselage
tank of the F-4E and various updated aircraft systems. Deliveries were by
air in US markings, changed to Israeli insignia in (it is unofficially reported)
Cyprus. Subsequently further batches of F-4Es were supplied, until the
total by the final delivery in October 1976 had reached 204. A further six
RF-4Es were acquired between March and May 1977 to complete the overall
acquisition at 216 aircraft (204 E plus 12 RF).

Active missions began in November 1969 with an attack on an SA-2
Guideline SAM site at Abu Sueir, Egypt. For the next five years the Phantoms
operated mainly in the surface attack role, taking out the hardest and most

strongly defended targets, especially where strong fighter opposition was expected. At the same time the high cost of the F-4E caused its selection to be carefully scrutinized for each task, and its utilization was considerably less than that of the ubiquitous A-4 force. For straightforward air combat against run-of-the-mill MiG-21s the Mirage IIICJ was preferred, the Phantom being used only when its long-range radar and AAMs were particularly needed. For the past decade there have been six Phantom squadrons, as there have been six A-4 squadrons, each with one or two RFs to carry out reconnaissance with cameras, side-looking radar, IRLS (infra-red linescan) and communications by digital link and HF single-sideband radio.

It is widely believed that the Chel Ha'Avir, with the help of IAI, Elta and other Israeli companies, have substantially modified the Phantoms. Among new armament fits are 30mm DEFA guns; Shafrir AAMs and possibly an ASM tailored especially for knocking out enemy SAM batteries. The latter was one of the main tasks of Phantoms in the Yom Kippur War, when no fewer than 33 were shot down, most by the deadly SAM-6 missiles. Today the Phantoms are much better protected against such weapons; indeed it would be logical if some were being rebuilt to the F-4G Wild Weasel II standard as dedicated electronic-warfare aircraft.

Below: Pilots in the Chel Ha'Avir will know what dare not be published here: which airbase has an elevated taxiway alongside the runway.

Above: An early (c1970) photo of F-4E No 634. Chel Ha'Avir Phantoms have seldom been seen carrying Sparrow AAMs and have operated almost entirely in the air-to-ground attack role.

Britten-Norman Islander

BN-2A Srs 2

Origin: Britten-Norman (now Pilatus Britten-Norman), Bembridge, UK.
Type: Light utility transport.
Engines: Two 260hp Lycoming O-540-E4C5 six-cylinder opposed.
Dimensions: Span (extended tips) 53ft 0in (16·15m); length 35ft 8in (10·87m); height 13ft 8in (4·16m); wing area (extended) 337sq ft (31·3m²).
Weights: Empty 3,588lb (1627kg); loaded 6,300lb (2858kg).
Performance: Maximum speed 170mph (273km/h); cruising speed 158mph (254km/h); service ceiling 14,600ft (4450m); range (with extended tips) 1,263 miles (2033km).
Armament: Provision in Defender version, but none in Chel Ha'Avir service.
History: First flight June 1965, (Srs 2) 1969.

The only light aircraft of British design to have achieved any kind of market in the past 20 years, the Islander is a neat all-metal transport of extremely simple design, one of its unusual features being the use of two doors on the left and a third on the right to give immediate access to up to ten seats. Thus no aisle is needed, and the fuselage can be slimmer, lighter and offer less drag. The fixed nosewheel landing gear is suited to the roughest possible airstrips and places the floor close to the ground in a level attitude. Maximum payload is normally 2,300lb (1043kg), and in most exported Islanders, including those in Israel, the range is extended by additional tanks housed in raked wingtips which increase span and lift and offer no increase in drag. The Chel Ha'Avir was donated two civil Islanders at the end of 1973. They are used as light transports and navigator trainers. So far as is known there has not been any move to buy the armed Defender.

Cessna Skywagon

Model 180

Origin: Cessna Aircraft, Wichita, Kansas.
Type: Light utility transport.
Engine: One 230hp Teledyne Continental O-470-U six-cylinder opposed.
Dimensions: Span 35ft 10in (10·92m); length 25ft 7½in (7·81m); height 7ft 9in (2·36m); wing area 174sq ft (16·16m²).
Weights: Empty 1,520lb (689kg);loaded 2,800lb (1270kg).
Performance: Maximum speed 170mph (274km/h);cruising speed 121mph (195km/h); service ceiling 17,700ft (5395m); range (max fuel with 45min reserve) 1,163 miles (1872km).
History: First flight (civil 180) 1952.

One of the long-established utility machines in the Cessna range, the 180 Skywagon was in production from 1953 until 1981. The cabin seats a pilot and up to five passengers, but the two examples used by the Chel Ha'Avir spent much of their time in light cargo transport with front-line items, spare parts and other urgent but modest loads. Drawbacks included tailwheel landing gear and absence of the glass-fibre Cargo Pack fitted under the fuselage of the more powerful Model 185, which almost reached the Chel Ha'Avir as the U-17B-CE supplied under the Military Assistance Program (no explanation is available why these were not supplied). Despite its problems the all-metal structure, reliability and low operating costs of the two Skywagons caused the Chel Ha'Avir to select Cessna as the supplier of its standard aircraft in this class, the choice falling on the U206.

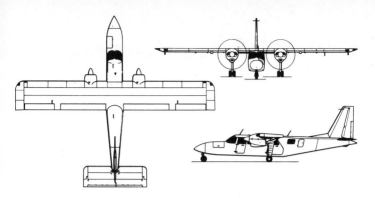

Above: Three-view of basic BN-2A Islander (without raked wingtips).

Below: One of the two BN-2As given to the Chel Ha'Avir in 1973.

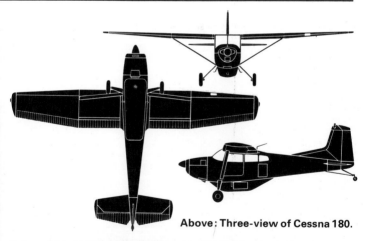

Above: Three-view of Cessna 180.

Below: This 180 has the same Service Number as the Islander above.

Cessna "Super Skywagon"
U206 Stationair and Model 172

Origin: Cessna Aircraft, Wichita, Kansas.
Type: Light utility transport.
Engine: One Teledyne Continental six-cylinder opposed, (206) 285hp IO-520-A, (172) 210hp IO-360-D.
Dimensions: Span (172) 35ft 10in (10·92m), (206) 36ft 7in (11·15m); length (172) 26ft 11in (8·2m), (206) 28ft 0in (8.53m); height 172) 8ft 9½in (2·68m), (206) 9ft 6¾in (2·92m); wing area (172) 174·0sq ft (16·17m²), (206) 175·5sq ft (16·3m²).
Weights: Empty (172) 1,394lb (632kg), (206) 1,780lb (807kg); loaded (172) 2,550lb (1157kg), (206) 3,300lb (1497kg).
Performance: Maximum speed (172) 156mph (251km/h), (206) 175mph (282km/h); cruising speed (typical for both) 131mph (211km/h); service ceiling (172) 17,000 ft (5180m), (206) 15,000ft (4570m); range (172) 1,010 miles (1625km), (206) 1,100 miles (1770km).
History: First flight (172) 1955, (206) 1964.

Grouped together for convenience in that both are single-engined Cessnas with tricycle landing gear, the 172 and 206 are very different in capacity, the former being at the most a four-seater (often less) and the 206 a full six-seater with provision for the patented detachable Cargo Pack. Only two Model 172s were used, both to the build standard of the USAF T-41D Mescalero primary pilot trainer. The U206 Stationair, however — always referred to in Israel by its former name of Super Skywagon — is one of the most numerous types in the entire Chel Ha'Avir. Exact numbers are not publishable, but possibly exceed 80. Unlike the earlier 180 the U206 has a level cabin floor on the ground, making it better suited to the casevac mission with two litter casualties. Both cargo doors can be removed for operations in the paradrop, photographic or other air/ground missions, though the normal role is that of a utility transport, able to carry a crate 4ft×3ft×3ft (1·15×0·91×0·91m) internally. Most have a large VHF/FM blade aerial above the cockpit.

Above: Three-view of Cessna 172/T-41D.

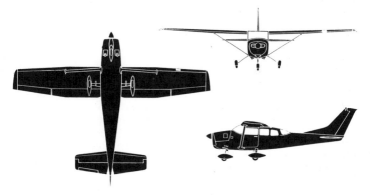

Above: Three-view of Cessna U206 "Super Skywagon".

Below: Normally equipped as six-seaters, the U206 serves in large numbers. The correct Cessna name is actually Stationair 6.

Bell 205

UH-1D series and AB 205

Origin: Bell Helicopter Textron, Fort Worth, Texas; AB 205 licence-built by CA Giovanni Agusta, Gallarate, Italy.
Type: Utility transport helicopter.
Engine: One 1,400hp Avco Lycoming T53-L-13 turboshaft flat-rated at 1,250hp.
Dimensions: Diameter of main rotor 48ft 0in (14·63m); length (ignoring rotors) 41ft 11in (12·78m); height 14ft 8in (4·48m); main-rotor disc area 1,809sq ft (168·06m²).
Weights: Empty about 4,800lb (2177kg); loaded (max) 9,500lb (4310kg).
Performance: (8,500lb, 3856kg) Maximum speed 138mph (222km/h); cruising speed 132mph (212km/h) hovering ceiling 11,000ft (3353m); range (max, no reserve) 360 miles (580km).
Armament: None usually fitted
History: First flight (XH-40) October 1956, (UH-1) 1958, (205) August 1961.

Most diverse and numerous of all helicopters, the so-called Huey family (the name comes from the original US Army designation of HU-1) is also in production in several sub-types at Agusta SpA in Italy as the AB 205, and Fuji in Japan (Bell and its foreign licensees had built almost 10,000 Model 205s by 1982.) The basic helicopter has a nose cockpit and main cabin providing 220cu ft (6·23m³) of clear space with twin doors on each side giving unrestricted access (in tactical roles these doors are often removed). Up to 14 troops can be carried, or six litter (stretcher) casualties and an attendant, or up to 3,880lb (1760kg) of cargo. Numerous options of special role equipment can be fitted, including various kinds of armament, but the UH-1D helicopters supplied from Texas to the Chel Ha'Avir are

Above: In the early 1970s it was often stated that the report that Israel used Agusta-Bell 205s was incorrect. In fact it uses both Bell- and Agusta-built 205s; this one is an AB 205.

Below: Three-view of Bell
205 with skid landing gear
but without powered hoist.

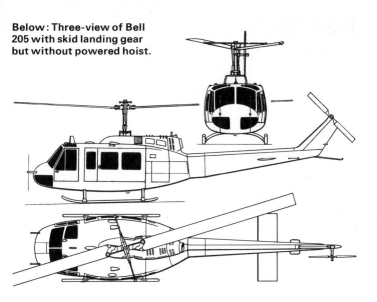

normally used in plain transport and troop assault roles. They are of basic UH-1D type, originally with US Army avionics, but in the past few years they have been progressively updated with numerous new avionic items, some of US Army types and others of local manufacture. The total number in the Chel Ha'Avir has been given as 25, 30, 34 and 45; another standard source gives the total as 23 Agusta-Bell AB 205 plus 20 Bell UH-1D. During the Rhodesian civil war 11 were passed on to the Rhodesian government, at least nine still being in Zimbabwe service.

Above: Still a very important type in the inventory, the Bell 205 has given good service in conditions like these. Note the special communications aerials and IR-supressed jetpipe.

Left: This Bell 205 has a powered hoist but no footsteps for the pilot and front-seat passenger (usually on the front of the landing skids).

Bell Twin Two-Twelve
Model 212/UH-1N

Origin: Bell Helicopter Textron, Fort Worth, Texas.
Type: VIP, liaison and rescue helicopter.
Engine: One 1,800hp Pratt & Whitney of Canada PT6T-3B twin turboshaft flat-rated at 1,290hp, with emergency power of 1,025hp available from either engine in event of failure of the other.
Dimensions: Diameter of main rotor 48ft $2\frac{1}{4}$in (14·69m); length (ignoring rotors) 57ft $3\frac{1}{4}$in (17·46m); height 14ft $10\frac{1}{4}$in (4·53m); main-rotor disc area 1,824sq ft (169·4m²).
Weights: Empty (VFR) 6,143lb (2786kg); loaded 11,200lb (5080kg).
Performance: Maximum speed 161mph (259km/h); cruising speed 142mph (228km/h); service ceiling 14,200ft (4330m); range (max, no reserve) 261 miles (420km).
Armament: None.
History: First flight 1969, (UH-1N) 1970.

One of the later sub-families within the vast Huey series, the Twin Two-Twelve was originally developed for the Canadian Armed Forces, the engine also being Canadian. The PT6T is a single package with two PT6 power sections each with a maximum power of some 1,000hp, but normally both operated together and restricted to a total combined power of 1,290hp. Thus even in the extreme heat and occasional elevated landing locations in Israel the 212 offers full performance, and the cabin is slightly enlarged compared with the Model 205 (248cu ft, 7·02m³) and provided with air conditioning for improved comfort. Though greater loads are possible the normal military cargo load limit is 4,000lb (1814kg), either inside or slung externally. The Chel Ha'Avir bought 12 of similar build standard to the US military UH-1N but subsequently updated with additional avionics. They are used for VIP liaison, rescue and special missions.

Below: So far as published photographs show, all Bell 212s in use have the hoist, used here in practice rescue operations.

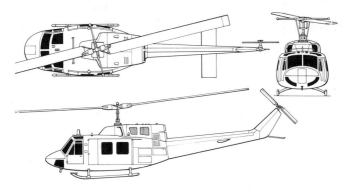

Above: Three-view of Bell 212 without external role equipment.

Above: A Chel Ha'Avir 212 setting down a package of front-line supplies for an M113 APC platoon somewhere in the desert.

Bell 209 HueyCobra
AH-1G, AH-1S

Origin: Bell Helicopter Textron, Fort Worth, Texas.
Type: Close support and attack helicopter.
Engine: One 1,400hp Avco Lycoming T53-L-13 turboshaft flat-rated at 1,100hp for continuous or hot/high operation; AH-1S, 1,800hp T53-L-703.
Dimensions: Diameter of main rotor 44ft 0in (13·41m); length (ignoring rotors) 44ft 7in (13·59m); height 13ft 6¼in (4·12m); main-rotor disc area 1,502·5sq ft (141·25m²).
Weights: Empty (including crew, armour, oil etc) 6,073lb (2755kg); loaded 9,500lb (4309kg).
Performance: Maximum speed 172mph (277km/h); speed limit in dives 219mph (352km/h); service ceiling 11,400ft (3475m); range (max fuel, 8 per cent reserve) 357 miles (574km).
Armament: One M28 turret under nose with (usually) one 7·62mm GE Minigun and one 40mm grenade launcher; stub wings carry four pylons for such loads as four M159 launchers (each 19 rockets of 2·75in calibre), M18E1 Minigun pods, chaff boxes or (if modification with large stabilized nose sight system is installed) two quad tubes for TOW guided missiles; AH-1S, 20mm M197 three-barrel gun.
History: First flight (209) September 1965, US combat service June 1967.

The result of a private development by Bell, the Model 209 came just as the large and complex AH-56A was suffering severe development problems, and the USA (and later the USN and USMC) bought it in very large numbers primarily for the anti-armour role. Following the Vietnam war numerous early AH-1G Cobras became surplus to requirements. Many were rebuilt as AH-1Q and TOW-equipped AH-1S models. In 1974 six were supplied to Israel, prior to any extensive rebuild programme. It is likely that additional quantities have been airlifted to Israel since 1974, but no announcement has been ·made. The original batch have unquestionably been updated after entry to Chel Ha'Avir service, in most cases by fitting the TOW anti-armour missile system which calls for a major reconstruction of the nose to accommodate the large tracking and sighting system. Other modifications made include fitting a flat-plate glass canopy over the pilot (rear seat) and co-pilot/gunner, special exhaust system to reduce infra-red signature and the addition of locally developed special mission avionics and armament options. A force of 12 would hardly be economically viable, and it is clear that the Chel Ha'Avir selection for its future close-support and attack helicopter is the smaller Hughes Defender.

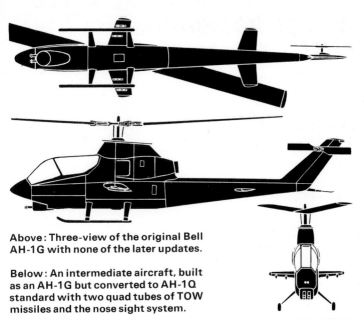

Above: Three-view of the original Bell AH-1G with none of the later updates.

Below: An intermediate aircraft, built as an AH-1G but converted to AH-1Q standard with two quad tubes of TOW missiles and the nose sight system.

Left: The latest Chel Ha'Avir Cobras are of this fully upgraded AH-1S type, with a bulletproof, non-distorting flat-plate cockpit canopy. Other features include the M197 three-barrel 20mm cannon, twin (as here) or quad TOW tubes and shrouded and upswept jetpipe to reduce the IR (infra-red) signature and thus offer some protection against SAMs.

Bell JetRanger
Model 206A, possibly 206B

Origin: Bell Helicopter Textron, Fort Worth, Texas.
Type: Liaison helicopter.
Engine: One 317hp Allison 250-C18 turboshaft.
Dimensions: Diameter of main rotor 33ft 4in (10·16m); length (ignoring rotors) 31ft 2in (9.50m); height 9ft 6½in (2·91m); main-rotor disc area 873sq ft (81·1m²).
Weights: Empty 1,407lb (638kg); loaded 3,000lb (1361kg).
Performance: Maximum speed 133mph (214km/h); cruising speed (max, at max wt) 122mph (196km/h); service ceiling (2,600lb, 1179kg) over 18,500ft (5640m); range (max wt, sea level) 362 miles (582km).
History: First flight January 1966.

Very widely used in civil and miltary forms, the original Model 206 Jet-Ranger has since been developed into Series I, II and III forms, the stretched LongRanger and armed TexasRanger, while military models are mainly known as OH-58 Kiowas (other variants include the TH-57A SeaRanger and CH-136). As far as is known all 20 of the Chel Ha'Avir fleet were basic commercial Model 206 JetRangers. These are normally equipped with a two-seat nose cockpit (dual flight controls are an option) and a rear bench seat for three, though in Israeli service some of the JetRangers have other arrangements including two rear VIP seats and an open rear cabin for special cargo. Deliveries began in about 1972, and one of the original batch is reported to have been destroyed by an SA-7 missile during the war in 1973. There have been several reports of a further batch, probably of the updated and more powerful Series II or III type, but no announcement has been made. Certainly, none of the armed Kiowa and TexasRanger models have been seen in Israel, all JetRangers being executive and liaison machines mainly used in place of the Alouettes.

Below: This example has ventral equipment and also a large mast/whip aerial, possibly for communication with ground forces.

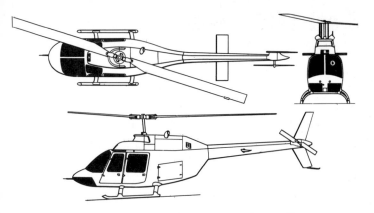

Above: Three-view of basic unarmed 206B JetRanger II.

Above: This JetRanger has a perforated engine bay cowl and a row of unexplained equipment along the fuselage underside.

Lockheed Hercules

C-130E, C-130H, KC-130H

Origin: Lockheed-Georgia Company, Marietta.
Type: Airlift transport, (KC) tanker/transport.
Engines: Four Allison single-shaft turboprops, (E) 4,050ehp T56-A-7, (H) 4,910ehp T56-A-15 flat-rated at 4,508ehp.
Dimensions: Span 132ft 7in (40·41m); length 97ft 9in (29·79m); height 38ft 3in (11·66m); wing area 1,745sq ft (162.1m²).
Weights: Empty (E) 72,892lb (33,064kg), (H) 75,741lb (34,356kg); loaded (E, H) normal 155,000lb (70,308kg), (overload) 175,000lb (79,380kg).
Performance: Maximum speed 384mph (618km/h); cruising speed 340mph (547km/h); service ceiling (E, 155,000lb, 70,308kg) 23,000ft (7010m); range (max payload), (E) 2,420 miles (3895km), (H) 2,450 miles (3943km); typical range (max fuel) 4,770 miles (7675km).
Armament: None.
History: First flight (YC-130) August 1954, (E) August 1961.

By far the most successful large military transport in history, the C-130 has outlived numerous replacements and has remained in full production for a growing list of customers for 30 years. They completely transformed the nation's long-range airlift capability.

Features of the basic C-130 include a fully pressurized fuselage with heating and air-conditioning, full-section rear ramp/doors for loading

Above: Infantry streaming from a C-130 (probably an E, with registration 4X-FBA). The unit badge on the fin is the same as that previously carried by the B-377 Stratocruisers.

Right: 4X-FBT is probably a C-130H, though with the Chel Ha'Avir wrong guesses are easy! Four Israeli C-130Hs, and two KC-130H tankers, made the daring rescue raid on Entebbe.

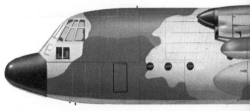

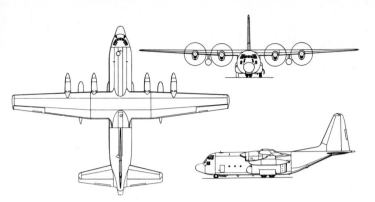

Above: Three-view of C-130E.

vehicles or large palletized freight or for airdropping large loads (or high-rate paratroop descent), a long-span high-lift wing, four main landing wheels with low-pressure tyres suitable for unpaved airstrips, a capacious cockpit with exceptional all-round view, nose radar, and outstanding flight performance and handling. From the start the C-130 was tremendously popular with flight and ground crews, and it was the first time all necessary features had been combined in a military transport. The basic payload is 45,525lb (20,650kg) for the C-130H, and very slightly less (45,000lb, 20,412kg) for the E. With the normal-length fuselage, as used by the Chel Ha'Avir, the maximum number of troop seats is 92. Seven standard pallets

Above: Slow run with partial flap by a C-130E with external fuel tanks. The same aircraft appears on page 127.

4X-FBT

of cargo can be loaded, and in the dedicated casevac role (very unlikely in Israel, where casevac does not require long range) the maximum number of stretcher (litter) patients is 70, with six attendants. The main cargo hold is 10ft 3in (3·13m) wide and 9ft 2¾in (2·81m) high, sufficient for most normal vehicles, artillery and light armour but unable to accept large ground radars, the heaviest trucks or (on size or weight grounds) a main battle tank.

Two initial C-130Hs were delivered to Israel at the end of 1971. At the outbreak of the Yom Kippur War in October 1973, a dozen C-130Es were rushed in. In that conflict the C-130s were intensively used for every kind of transport mission, but none was lost. After that war a further 6 aircraft of the more powerful C-130H type were received, delivered new from the production line. The force was completed by two KC-130H tankers with additional transfer fuel in the fuselage and an inflight refuelling hosereel pod under each outer wing. Four C-130H were used on the daring and highly successful Entebbe raid on 4 July 1976 which rescued 103 airline passengers held hostage by terrorists who had hijacked an A300B2 Airbus. This mission involved a secret flight to the extreme range of which the C-130 was capable, yet all four returned safely to Israel.

Below: An immaculate Chel Ha'Avir C-130 (probably an H) on a visit to Frankfurt Rhein-Main airport. The assisted-takeoff rocket attachments behind the gear fairings have never been used.

Above: Another view of an earlier C-130, 4X-FBB. One can just
discern the downward-slanting smoke trails from the four jetpipes,
a characteristic of the C-130 (and of the similar An-12).

Sikorsky S-65
S-65C-3 (CH-53D), CH-53Öe

Origin: Sikorsky Aircraft Division of United Technologies, Stratford, Connecticut.
Type: Heavy airlift helicopter.
Engines: Two 3,925hp General Electric T64 turboshafts, (C-3) T64-GE-413, (Öe) T64-GE-7.
Dimensions: Diameter of main rotor 72ft 3in (22·02m); length (ignoring rotors and refuelling probe) 67ft 2in (20·47m); height 24ft 11in (7·60m); main-rotor disc area 4,070sq ft (378·1m²).
Weights: Empty 23,485lb (10,653kg); loaded (max) 42,000lb (19,050kg).
Performance: Maximum speed 196mph (315km/h); cruising speed 173mph (278km/h); service ceiling 21,000ft (6400m); range (with reserves) 257 miles (413km).
Armament: None known in Israeli service.
History: First flight (CH-53A) October 1964; delivery of first CH-53D to US Marine Corps March 1969.

The Israeli Chel Ha'Avir had obviously studied the S-65 from the earliest days of this extremely capable helicopter, which in the course of 20 years of development has grown in capability from two engines of 2,850hp in the CH-53A to three engines of 4,380hp in the CH-53E. The Israeli examples are of two almost identical types in between the first and most recent examples, still with two engines but considerably more powerful than in the CH-53A and giving good all-round performance even in high altitude conditions at very high ambient temperature. The S-65C-3 was a commercial designation applied to a helicopter virtually identical to the Marine Corps CH-53D and included in the USMC purchases, afterwards being transferred to Israel without announcement. The number of this version is

Above: A 1977 picture of an S-65C-3 with engine-inlet filters.

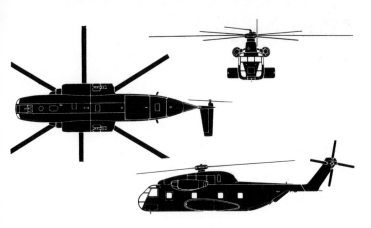

Above: Three-view of original S-65 without inlet sand filters.

variously given as 20 and "about 25". They were flown in, probably by C-5A, from autumn 1969.

On 26 December 1969 a special-mission force was carried in two of the new helicopters to Ras Ghareb, some 115 miles (185km) south of Suez on the Gulf of Suez shore, where a complete Soviet-installed P-50 air-defence radar (NATO codename Bar Lock) was captured and the operative sections dismantled and flown to Israel. The helicopters brought back the entire main van portions and the pair of giant parabolic aerials.

All the S-65 helicopters have armour, jettisonable long-range tanks (not allowed for in the range figures above) and have been retrofitted with inflight-refuelling probes. It has been reported in the Press that in 1981 Israel purchased the two S-65Öe of the Austrian Air Force. The report that 18 CH-53G were bought from Federal Germany is without foundation.

Above: A fine study of CH-53 No 552 with landing gear extended. All carry drop tanks and a probe.

Left: Though most are S-65C-3s the common designation used in Israel is CH-53. This is No 247.

Boeing 707

707-124, -131, -321, -328 and -329

Origin: The Boeing Company, Seattle.

Type: Variously used as transport, command centre, tanker and other special roles.

Engines: Originally JT3C, JT3D, JT4A; believed now all 18,000lb (8165kg) Pratt & Whitney JT3D-3 turbofans.

Dimensions: Span (124, 131) 130ft 10in (39·88m), (320) 142ft 5in (43·41m); (320) 145ft 9in (44·42m); length (excluding boom if fitted) (131) 144ft 6in (44·04m), (320) 152ft 11in (46·61m); height (131) 42ft 0in (12·8m), (320) 42ft 5in (12·93m); wing area (131) 2,433sq ft (226·03m²), (320) 3,010sq ft (279·63m²).

Weights (approx): Empty (131) 124,000lb (56,246kg), (320) 141,200lb (64,048kg); loaded (131) 257,000lb (116,575kg), (320) 333,600lb (151,320kg).

Performance: Maximum speed (typical) 627mph (1009km/h); cruising speed (typical) 540mph (869km/h); max cruising height 39,000ft (11,887 m); range (max payload, no reserves) (131) 3,217 miles (5177km), (320) 6,160 miles (9915km).

History: First flight (Dash-80 prototype) July 1954, (production -121) December 1957, (-320) January 1959.

No Boeing 707 was supplied new to the Chel Ha'Avir, but so many commercial 707s, of so many types, have passed through the hands of Israeli organizations — notably IAI at Lod Airport which besides overhauling aircraft for other operators also does a brisk buying, selling and leasing business — that it is not easy to determine how many have seen Israeli air force service. The slick answer is that the total is ten, some of them ex-TWA 707-131s originally built with JT3C engines and with the small airframe, and the others 707-320s acquired from European airlines. The first 707s entered Chel Ha'Avir service during the Yom Kippur War. To make it more difficult at least one ex-Sabena -329 with the larger but older airframe and JT4A turbojet engines and two ex-Continental -124s in the original small

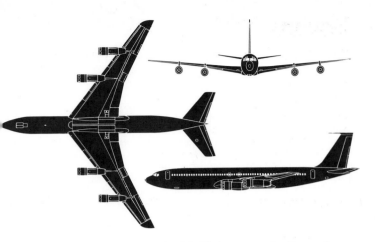

Above: Three-view of 707-320C with Küchemann wingtips and JT3D-3 turbofan engines.

series have also served with the Israeli government, the two -124s in Chel Ha'Avir units. With the obvious difficulty of tight security it is impossible to resolve the problem, but there is no doubt that today the large 707 Intercontinental type is serving in passenger/cargo transport, electronic warfare, mobile command centre and special communications roles, whilst at least five of the smaller (ex-124 or -131) models are serving as dedicated tankers with KC-135 boom installations for serving F-15s and F-16s. One of the larger machines served as a fully equipped surgical hospital at Nairobi ready to receive the returning wounded from the Entebbe raid of 4 July 1976.

Below: Possibly the Israeli equivalent of "Air Force One", this 707-320 (not -320C) was powered by JT4A turbojets in the mid-1970s but has since received JT3Ds. Note the dorsal blade aerials.

IAI Kfir

Salvo, Nesher, Kfir-C1, -C2 and -TC2

Origin: Israel Aircraft Industries, Lod Airport.
Type: Multi-role fighter and attack, (TC-2) trainer and EW.
Engine (except Nesher): One 17,900lb (8119kg) General Electric J79-J1E augmented turbojet.
Dimensions: (Nesher) as Mirage CJ, (Kfir) span 26ft $11\frac{1}{2}$in (8·22m); length (C1, C2) 51ft $4\frac{1}{4}$in (15·65m), (C2 with Elta radar) 53ft $11\frac{3}{4}$in (16·45m); (TC2) 54ft $1\frac{1}{4}$in (16·49m); height 14ft $11\frac{1}{4}$in (4·55m); wing area 374·6 sq ft (34·8m²); foreplane 17·87sq ft (1·66m²).
Weights: (Kfir) Empty (C2, interceptor) 16, 060lb (7285kg); loaded (C2, half internal fuel plus two Shafrir) 20,700lb (9390kg), (C2, max with full internal fuel, two tanks, seven 500lb bombs and two Shafrir) 32,340lb (14,670kg).
Performance: (C2) Maximum speed (clean) 863mph (1389km/h) at sea level, over Mach 2·3 (1,516mph, 2440km/h) above 36,090ft (11km); initial climb 45,950ft/min (233m/s); service ceiling 58,000ft (17,680m); combat radius (20min reserve), (interceptor, two 110gal, 500 litre tanks plus two Shafrir) 215 miles (346km), (attack, three 330gal, 1500 litre tanks plus seven bombs and two Shafrir, hi-lo-hi) 477 miles (768km).
Armament: Two IAI-built DEFA 5-52 guns each with 140 rounds; seven hardpoints for total of 9,469lb (4295kg) of various stores, always including two Shafrir 2 AAMs (outer wings) plus tanks, bombs (ten 500lb, 227kg), Luz-1 missiles, Maverick or Hobos missiles, rocket pods, Matra Durandal or other anti-runway weapons, napalm, ECM pods and tanks.
History: First flight (Nesher) reportedly September 1969, (Salvo) September 1970, (C1 prototype) 1972, (production C1) 1974, (C2) 1975, (TC2) February 1981.

Though Israel may not have foreseen the rather sudden switch-around in the attitude of France in the summer of 1973, work aimed at eventually giving Israel the capability of building fighters was initiated as early as 1969. In that year IAI began a study project named Black Curtain to investigate the possibility of fitting the J79 engine, as used in the F-4E, into a Mirage.

Below: This aircraft is believed to have been the first Kfir-C2. Yellow wing triangles were later copied by the Egyptian AF.

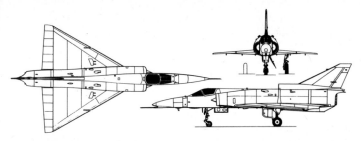

Above: Three-view of IAI Kfir before conversion to C2 standard.

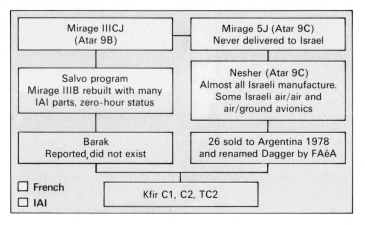

Mirage IIICJ (Atar 9B)	Mirage 5J (Atar 9C) Never delivered to Israel
Salvo program Mirage IIIB rebuilt with many IAI parts, zero-hour status	Nesher (Atar 9C) Almost all Israeli manufacture. Some Israeli air/air and air/ground avionics
Barak Reported, did not exist	26 sold to Argentina 1978 and renamed Dagger by FAéA

☐ French
☐ IAI

Kfir C1, C2, TC2

Above: Simplified guide to the evolutionary process leading to the Kfir. It is unlikely to be taken any further.

Though there were many problems these were solved or bypassed, in a somewhat imperfect J79 installation. The trial installation was made in a Mirage IIIBJ named Salvo with rear cockpit occupied by an engineer monitoring test instrumentation; this flew in September 1970 and was valuable in highlighting faults and deficiencies.

While this was in its early stages Israel obtained by clandestine sources manufacturing drawings for the Mirage 5 and (from an employee of

SNECMA's licensee Sulzer Brothers in Switzerland) the Atar 9C, a slightly more advanced engine than the 9B used in the Chel Ha'Avir Mirage IIIs. These plans, a remarkable coup in industrial espionage, immediately prompted the manufacture of the Atar-powered Mirage, avoiding all the many problems attendant upon the installation of the J79. The decision was taken to tool up for production of an Atar-powered Mirage, with the name Nesher (Eagle), the first flying in September 1969. Several had flown in 1971 and the first Chel Ha'Avir Nesher unit was formed in 1972. It was reported that about 40 took part in the Yom Kippur War. Their radar was an Elta-built improved version of the original Cyrano, which had previously been made under CSF licence, though some Neshers had no radar but only a simple radar ranging sight, based on Aida II. The Neshers appear to be the aircraft subsequently sold to Argentina.

The performance advantages of the J79 engine resulted in further development based on the Mirage 5 airframe leading to the definitive Kfir (Lion Cub). This offered more internal fuel, much better weapon capability and more than 270 engineering changes compared with the Nesher, the engine installation being based on the Salvo. The Kfir has a modified inlet system, enlarged ducts, a new engine bay of reduced length, a new dorsal fin with ram inlet, four further engine-bay cooling inlets, completely revised cockpit, new nose with basically triangular section, new fuel system with

Above: The tandem-seat Kfir-TC2 appears to have sagged in the heat, but in fact flight testing confirmed no speed reduction.

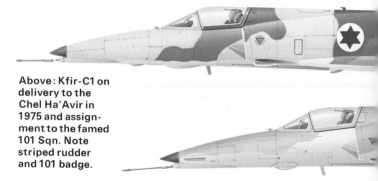

Above: Kfir-C1 on delivery to the Chel Ha'Avir in 1975 and assignment to the famed 101 Sqn. Note striped rudder and 101 badge.

greater capacity than the Mirage 5, strengthened longer-stroke main landing gears and totally new avionics of mainly Israeli origin. The Kfir-C1 entered production in 1974 as a multi-role air superiority and ground-attack fighter. The first two aircraft were delivered to the Chel Ha'Avir in June 1975.

Further development led to the Kfir-C2, with major aerodynamic and avionics improvements. Adding small strakes along the sides of the nose and removable (but fixed-incidence) foreplanes above the inlets dramatically improved low-speed and combat-manoeuvre capability, which was further enhanced by extending the outer wing leading edges with a sharp dogtooth at the inner end of the added portion. The C2 has shorter takeoff and landing, steeper landing approach in a flatter attitude and markedly better combat agility, including reduced gust response in low-level attack. The C2 was revealed at Hatzerim in July 1976, when it was announced as available for export at some $5m. The various improvements are believed to have been incorporated in surviving C1 aircraft. The standard C2 has an extended nose housing the Elta EL/M-2001B ranging radar. Standard C2 equipment includes inertial navigation, very comprehensive flight-control and weapon-delivery systems and a high standard of EW/ECM installations. Further subsystems are in the rear cockpit of the two-seat TC2 version, first flown in 1981, with a distinctive down-sloping extended nose. By 1982 about 220 Kfirs had been delivered including several to Colombia.

Below: Kfir-C2 in air-superiority two-tone grey scheme adopted in 1978.

IAI Arava

IAI 101, 201

IAI 101, 201
Origin: Israel Aircraft Industries, Lod Airport.
Type: Light STOL utility transport.
Engines: Two 750hp Pratt & Whitney of Canada PT6A-34 turboprops.
Dimensions: Span 68ft 9in (20·96m); length 42ft 9in (13·03m); height 17ft 1in (5·21m); wing area 470·2sq ft (43·68m²).
Weights: (201) Empty (basic operating) 8,816lb (3999kg); loaded 15,000lb (6804kg).
Performance: Maximum speed 203mph (326km/h); cruising speed 193mph (311km/h); service ceiling 25,000ft (7620m); range (max payload, 45 min reserves) 174 miles (280km), (max fuel, 45min reserves) 812 miles (1306km).
Armament: (201) provision for two forward-firing 0·5in (12·7mm) guns in fuselage-side packs, plus pylons for two rocket pods each for six 82mm calibre; additional hand-aimed 0·5in gun mounted on pintle at rear of nacelle if required.
History: First flight (101) November 1969, (201) March 1972.

The first major aircraft designed entirely in Israel, the Arava is a substantial all-metal STOL transport to have maximum versatility in civil or military operations. Powered by two well-proven turboprops mounted on a high-lift wing with long-span double-slotted flaps, small ailerons and spoilers, the Arava carries its load in a short but capacious nacelle of circular cross-section (though it is unpressurized). The fixed nosewheel-type landing gear is mounted on the nacelle, and the tail is carried on two slender booms. The flight deck is fitted for one or two pilots; the main cabin can seat 20 passengers, or 24 troops, or 17 paratroops plus dispatcher, or provide 12 stretchers (litters) plus two sitting patients and attendant, or 5,184lb (2351kg) of cargo which can include light vehicles driven in with the rear of the nacelle swung open. The Chel Ha'Avir adopted a negative attitude at the start, emphasizing its commitment to the old C-47 and its disinterest in IAI's search for markets. By 1972 IAI was selling to various foreign military customers, the 201 being offered with a wealth of weapons, avionics,

Below: Ground crew, flight crew and infantry with one of the commandeered Aravas during the 1973 Yom Kippur War.

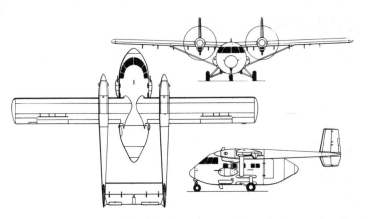

Above: Three-view of IAI-201 Arava (gun packs and stores pylons).

sensors, palletized ESM/ECM/Elint installations, maritime surveillance and other special role kits. Then came the Yom Kippur war, and the Chel Ha'Avir commandeered the second 101 and a pair of military 201s built for an export customer. They were used for front-line supply and casevac missions, but were returned to the original customers. The Chel Ha'Avir does not operate Aravas today.

Above: Driving a Ramta 4x4 "Jeep" into an Arava using light ramps. For air-dropping the nacelle tail is removed.

Grumman Mohawk

OV-1D

Origin: Grumman Aerospace Corporation, Bethpage, NY.
Type: Reconnaissance and electronic intelligence (Elint) aircraft.
Engines: Two 1,400hp Avco Lycoming T53-L-701 turboprops flat-rated at 1,160hp.
Dimensions: Span 48ft 0in (14·63m); length (excluding avionics) 41ft 0in (12·50m); height 12ft 8in (3·86m); wing area 360sq ft (33·45m²).
Weights: Empty about 12,100lb (5489kg); loaded (max) 18,250lb (8278kg).
Performance: Maximum speed 285mph (459km/h); cruising speed 207mph (333km/h); service ceiling 25,000ft (7620m); range (max, drop tanks) 944 miles (1520km); endurance at 161mph (259km/h), 4hr 21min.
History: First flight (YOV-1) April 1959, (RV-1D) 1981.

This unique STOL twin-turboprop was developed in the late 1950s to meet a US Army need for a high-performance observation aircraft. Several variants matured, adding to the eyes of the crew of two an increasing range of sensors including optical cameras, infra-red linescan and side-looking airborne radar (SLAR). In recent years Grumman has rebuilt some 80 earlier Mohawks to bring them up to OV-1D standard with the choice of IR or SLAR for each mission. Continuing operational demands led to further variants,

Below: It proved impossible to prise a Mohawk picture out of Israel, but this will do almost as well. It is possible that the Chel Ha'Avir will receive the Elint EV-1E or RV-1D version.

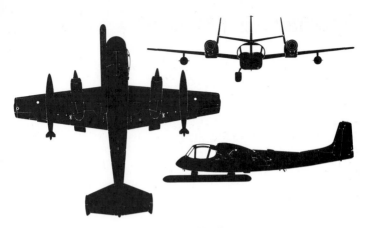

Above: Three-view of OV-1D with SLAR.

including the RV-1D (OV-1B rebuilt for tac-recon) and the more extensively reconfigured EV-1E. Originally OV-1Ds, these 16 aircraft have been completely re-equipped for electronic intelligence (Elint) missions. They carry ALQ-133 (Quick Look II) surveillance radar and new ventral and wingtip pods for recording and classifying all hostile emissions and their locations. Two OV-1Ds were delivered to the Chel Ha'Avir in 1974. There has been widespread confusion caused by reports of RV-1D aircraft being in service in Israel, but official records indicate that these two OV-1D Mohawks are the only examples of this basic type in the Chel Ha'Avir.

McDonnell Douglas F-15 Eagle

F-15A, F-15B, F-15C

Origin: McDonnell Aircraft Co, St Louis.
Type: Fighter, with secondary attack role.
Engines: Two Pratt & Whitney F100-PW-100 augmented turbofans each rated at 14,670lb (6654kg) dry and 23,830lb (10,809kg) with maximum afterburner.
Dimensions: Span 42ft 9¾in (13·05m); length 63ft 9in (19·43m); height 18ft 5½in (5·63m); wing area 608sq ft (56·5m²).
Weights: Empty (basic equipped) 28,000lb (12,700kg); loaded (interceptor with four Sparrows and full internal fuel) 41,500lb (18,824kg); maximum (attack or ferry) 56,500lb (25,628kg).
Performance: Maximum speed 1,648mph (2652km/h, Mach 2·5) above 36,000ft, 11km; service ceiling about 65,000ft (19·8km); range on internal fuel (clean) 2,878 miles (4630km).
Armament: One 20mm M61A-1 six barrel gun with 940 rounds; four AIM-7F (or other model) Sparrow AAMs carried against chines of fuselage and four AIM-9L or Shafrir close-range AAMs in pairs under wing, plus

Above: One of the original batch of F-15As, with tank and maximum AAMs.

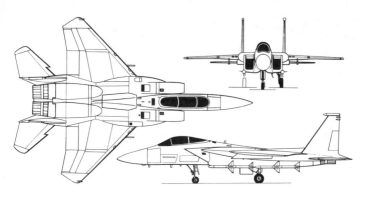

Above: Three-view of F-15A (15C similar) with Sparrows only.

provision for five pylons for tanks, ECM pods or other loads including bombs or rockets to total mass of 16,000lb (7258kg).

History: First flight July 1972; service delivery (USAF) November 1974.

Generally rated as the world's top air-superiority aircraft, the F-15 was the end-product of an FX programme started in 1965 to find an answer to the Soviet MiG-25 (a totally different species of aircraft with an unrivalled

Above: Flying at about 1,000ft (300m) altitude in an echelon of Israeli Eagles. The photograph was taken by the back-seater in an F-15B, and aircraft No 704 is also an F-15B. What a contrast to the Avia S 199s!

straight-line performance but no dogfight capability whatever). Though slower, the F-15 is an all-round multi-mission aircraft, though its wing is sized for close air combat and is far too large for comfortable low-level attack except at much-reduced speed. This is not much problem to the Chel Ha'Avir which has always regarded the F-15 in an air-superiority context.

An Israeli contract was delayed partly by uncertainty on the part of the customer and partly by reluctance on the part of the vendor, who wished to avoid causing a storm in the Arab world. For about five years the size, possible vulnerability and astronomic cost of the F-15 made it less than attractive to many Chel Ha'Avir pilots and generals, but the sheer capability of the aircraft in so many scenarios and missions eventually led to a decision in 1975 to purchase 48. Within months this was rescinded, the order being cut back to 25 in order to release funds for F-16s. Owing to the acute Middle East political situation the US government authorized a programme called Peace Fox under which delivery was brought forward from 1977 to 1976, mainly by getting McDonnell to refurbish seven of the 20 development air-

craft (which had not been intended for delivery to a service customer) and bring them up as nearly as possible to F-15A standard. Deliveries started, by air, in USAF markings, on 10 December 1976. All 25 of the original order, costing a reported $600 million, were delivered by the end of 1977. They are said to equip No 133 Sqn, though the Chel Ha'Avir is sensitive to unit identities. Their performance has been all that was expected, and in numerous brief clashes with hostile (mainly Syrian) aircraft they have scored several confirmed kills without loss. Their main role has been area-defence top cover, working in conjunction with the E-2Cs. By 1982 a further 15 Eagles, believed to be F-15Cs with extra fuel and improved avionics had been added to the inventory, and a third batch of 11 aircraft had been ordered, making 51 in all.

Below: A fine study of No 672, almost certainly an F-15C, taken in 1981. The aircraft is absolutely clean (apart from flaps and airbrake) with no pylons, Fast (fuel and sensor) packs or AAMs.

IAI Westwind

IAI 1123, 1124N Sea Scan

Origin: Israel Aircraft Industries, Lod Airport.
Type: (1123) jet liaison, (1124N) maritime patrol.
Engines: (1123) two 3,100lb (1406kg) General Electric CJ610-9 turbojets, (1124N) two 3,700lb (1678kg) Garrett TFE 731-3-1G turbofans with reversers.
Dimensions: Span (over tanks) 44ft 9½in (13·65m); length (1123) 52ft 3in (15·93m), (N) 55ft 1in (16·79m); height 15ft 9½in (4·81m); wing area 308·26sq ft (28·64m²).
Weights: Empty (1123) 9,370lb (4250kg), (N) 10,290lb (4667kg); loaded (1123) 20,700lb (9390kg), (N) 23,500lb (10,660kg).
Performance: Maximum speed 542mph (872km/h); cruising speed 420mph (676km/h); service ceiling 45,000ft (13,716m); range (1123, max payload, 45min reserves) 1,600 miles (2575km), (N, hi altitude) 3,339 miles (5373km), (N, lo-level search) 1,588 miles (2555km).
Armament: (1123) none, (N) torpedoes or Gabriel III anti-ship missiles.
History: First flight (Jet Commander) January 1963, (IAI Westwind) September 1970, (N) August 1978.

The Westwind is a very attractive executive jet descended from the American Jet Commander. IAI improved this into the 1121 Commodore Jet and thence into the 1123 Westwind with a longer cabin seating up to ten in addition to the two-seat cockpit, more powerful CJ610 engines, wingtip tanks, double-slotted flaps, an APU and many other changes. The Chel Ha'Avir first introduced two 1123 Westwinds into service during the Yom Kippur War in October 1973. One of these remains in use as a VIP transport, while the second and two additional Westwinds were converted in 1978–81 into Model 1124N Sea Scan offshore aircraft for the Israeli Navy. The Sea Scan is an extremely well equipped patrol aircraft with Litton APS-504(V) radar, Omega/VLF navigation, bubble windows, stores pylons and such additional sensor options as FLIR (forward-looking infra-red), LLTV (low-light TV) and MAD (magnetic-anomaly detection). Weapon options are listed above. The three Sea Scans are used day and night to guard the coast against sea landings by terrorists, such as the one in March 1978 in which 30 Israelis and tourists were massacred.

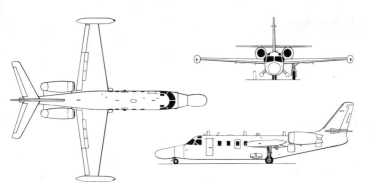

Above: Three-view of IAI 1124N Sea Scan.

Above: In 1977 the Israeli Navy bought three specially equipped 1123 Westwind 1s. They were later converted to 1124N Sea Scans.

Below: One of the three IAI 1124N Sea Scan offshore patrol aircraft, wearing on its tail the same badge seen on Stratocruisers, C-130s, 707s and other large Chel Ha'Avir transport aircraft.

Grumman Hawkeye

E-2C

Origin: Grumman Aerospace Corporation, Bethpage, NY.
Type: Airborne early-warning surveillance.
Engines: Two 4,910ehp Allison T56-A-425 turboprops.
Dimensions: Span 80ft 7in (24·56m); length 57ft 6¾in (17·54m); height 18ft 3¾in (5·58m); wing area 700sq ft (65·03m²).
Weights: Empty 37,945lb (17,212kg); loaded 51,817lb (23,504kg).
Performance: Maximum speed 374mph (602km/h); service ceiling 30,800ft (9390m); ferry range 1,605 miles (2583km); time on station 200 miles (322km) from base, 4h; max endurance 6h 6min.
History: First flight (W2F prototype) October 1960, (E-2C) January 1971.

Though it was designed for carrier operation, and with outer wings folded is remarkably compact, the E-2C Hawkeye has also been carefully marketed for overland use and has been sold to several air forces including the Chel Ha'Avir which purchased four, delivered in mid-1978. The main radar is the General Electric APS-125 which incorporates the ARPS (advanced radar processing subsystem) to increase sensitivity in noise and clutter, provide sophisticated false-alarm control and major ECCM (electronic counter-countermeasures). It also now uses digital MTI (moving-target indication) and has many other recent advances to give really effective surveillance over land or sea within a 3 million cubic mile volume, with detection and threat-

Above: At low levels the E-2C can be thrown about in lively fashion, though this is very rarely done.

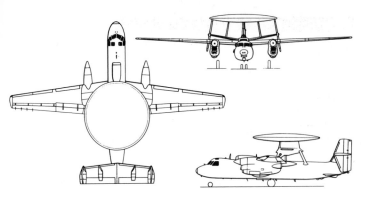

Above: Three-view of E-2C Hawkeye.

assessment of hostile aircraft out to almost 300 miles (480km) whilst continuing to monitor surface activity. The normal crew comprises the pilot and co-pilot, combat information centre officer, air control officer and radar operator. Though they cost well over $40 million each the four Hawkeyes have at last given Israel security against most forms of military attack, and enable the Chel Ha'Avir — and land and sea forces — to be deployed to maximum efficiency and effectiveness. There is a possibility two more may be acquired.

Above: For two years no Service Numbers appeared on the Hawkeyes, nor any unit badges, though there are plenty of stencilled instructions (which, unusually in the Chel Ha'Avir, are all in English only). Parked behind this example (now No 946) are Magister No 122, A-4E No 806 and a Phantom.

Left: E-2C profile.

General Dynamics F-16 Fighting Falcon

F-16A, F-16B

Origin: General Dynamics, Fort Worth Division, Fort Worth, Texas.

Type: Multi-role tactical fighter.

Engine: One Pratt & Whitney F100-PW-200 augmented turbofan rated at 14,670lb (6654kg) dry and 23,830lb (10,809kg) with maximum afterburner.

Dimensions: Span (over AAMs) 32ft 10in (10·01m) (without AAMs, 31ft 0in, 9·45m); length 49ft 6in (15·09m) (excluding nose probe, 47ft 7$\frac{3}{4}$in, 14·52m); height 16ft 5$\frac{1}{2}$in (5·01m); wing area 300sq ft (27·87m²).

Weights: Empty (F-16A) 15,586lb (7070kg), (B) 16,258lb (7374kg); loaded (A, interceptor, no tanks) 23,810lb (10,800kg), (both, max external load) 35,400lb (16,057kg).

Performance: Maximum speed (A, with AAMs only) 1,350mph (2170 km/h, Mach 2·05) at 40,000ft (12·2km) 915mph (1472km/h, Mach 1·2) at sea level; service ceiling, over 50,000ft (15,240m); tactical radius (hi-lo-hi mission with six Mk 82 bombs and no external fuel) 340 miles (550km); ferry range, more than 2,415 miles (3890km).

Armament: One 20mm M61A-1 gun with 515 rounds; two AIM-9L or Shafrir close-range AAMs on wingtip shoes; seven additional hardpoints stressed at 2,205lb/1000kg (centreline), 4,500lb/2041kg (inboard wing), 3,500lb/1588kg (centre underwing) and 700lb/318kg (under tip) for total load of 12,000lb (5443kg) at 9g factor and at reduced manoeuvre factor for limit of 20,450lb (9276kg).

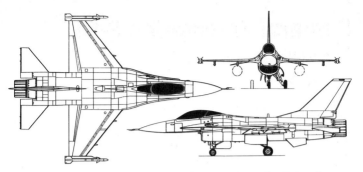

Above: Three-view of F-16A (nozzle open and small tailplane).

History: First flight (YF-16 official maiden flight) 2 February 1974, (production F-16A) 7 August 1978.

In the author's opinion the most cost/effective combat aircraft in the modern world, the F-16 began life as a mere technology demonstrator to see what capabilities could be provided in a small fighter cheaper than the large F-15. From the original GD Model 401 came the USAF YF-16 day fighter proto-type which after a flyoff against the twin-engined Northrop YF-17 was selected for full-scale development in 1975. Sudden emergence of a large NATO market resulted in urgent reappraisal of the programme, and in a matter of weeks the F-16A had become a multi-role all-weather platform being bought in numbers far exceeding the F-15 for the USAF and which has since sold to eight further countries with several additional nations in negotiation.

Left: The very quick delivery of F-16s to the Chel Ha'Avir was made possible partly by the cancellation of a large order by Iran and partly by the ability of the multi-national production programme to divert early deliveries to Israel. As a result the F-16A was combat-ready in Israel in 1980, and flew an operational bombing mission in June 1981. Substantial numbers of F-16s were used in the anti-PLO campaign in the Lebanon during June–July 1982. This air-craft, No 138, is painted in the sand overland scheme (sand/tan only), and has AIM-9J type Sidewinder AAMs. Unit badge censored.

Israel announced its intention to purchase the F-16 in August 1977, unusually announcing a planned total of 75 including eight of the tandem dual F-16B version, which has full combat capability within the same dimensions but 17 per cent less internal fuel. In structure, aerodynamics, systems (especially avionics architecture and philosophy), cockpit and many other respects the F-16 pushes ahead into a new era, and it is probably the most exciting and pleasurable military aircraft to fly in all history. Those who scorned its all-weather navigation and attack capability were startled when a team from the 388th TFW, USAF, won the RAF tac-bombing contest in 1981 with a score of 7,831 out of 8,000 (far and away the all-time record), beating Jaguars and F-111s in the process. At almost the same time, on 7 June 1981, eight of the Chel Ha'Avir aircraft flew from Etzion AB in the Sinai a distance of some 600 miles (966km) with pairs of 2,000lb (907kg) bombs, without air refuelling, to destroy the Osirak nuclear reactor in Iraq, which was a potential source of weapon-grade plutonium. By October 1981 all the Israeli aircraft had been delivered. Following the Israeli invasion of the Lebanon in June 1982, President Reagan embargoed a second batch of 75.

Above: In contrast to the previous page, this F-16A has regular camouflage.

Left: Plan view of F-16A No 105. Flight-refuelling boom receptacle (dorsal amidships) is retained.

Below: Much of the early training of F-16 air and ground crews was done at Hill Air Force Base, Utah, home of the most experienced (388th) F-16 Tac Fighter Wing. This F-16B two-seater was photographed there in 1981, painted with a USAF number as well as that of the Chel Ha'Avir.

Hughes Defender
500MD/TOW

Origin: Hughes Helicopters (subsidiary of Hughes Corporation), Culver City, California.
Type: Anti-armour helicopter.
Engine: One 420hp Allison 250-C20B turboshaft.
Dimensions: Diameter of main rotor 26ft 4¾in (8·05m); length (ignoring rotors) 23ft 0in (7·01m); height (over tail) 8ft 10¾in (2·71m); main-rotor disc area 545sq ft (50·63m²).
Weights: Empty 1,130lb (512kg); loaded (normal) 2,550lb (1157kg), (overload) 3,000lb (1361kg).
Performance: Maximum speed 152mph (245km/h); cruising speed 135mph (217km/h); service ceiling 14,400ft (4390m); range 366 miles (589km).
Armament: Two pairs of TOW missiles carried in left/right twin pods; many other options in later or different models, some of which may have been incorporated (such as twin Stinger anti-aircraft missiles, rocket pods, 7·62mm Minigun, 30mm Chain Gun or 40mm grenade launcher).
History: First flight (OH-6A) February 1963, (production 500D) October 1975.

Amazingly light and compact, the Model 500MD Defender is a family of advanced military models derived from the civil Model 500, which in turn was developed from the original lower-powered OH-6A Cayuse built in

Below: Looking almost like a four-jet aircraft with its two pairs of TOW missiles, this 500MD has Chel Ha'Avir number 207.

Above: Subject of the profile at left, this 500MD is being flown really low, as it must be in order to stay alive over the modern battlefield. The only drawback is that with a nose-mounted sight it is essential to rise up into view of the enemy in order to find targets and guide TOW missiles. Later 500MD Defenders have a mast-mounted sight which overcomes this problem. It could later be a retrofit.

Above: Standard Israeli 500MD with nose-mounted sight for TOW system.

Above: The Chel Ha'Avir Defenders have Black Hole Ocarina (IR-suppressed) engine exhaust stacks to reduce heat emissions.

numbers for the USA in the 1960s. The USA has not adopted any of the 500MD versions but they have sold to other operators all over the world and been licensed to BredaNardi (Italy), RACA (Argentina), Kawasaki (Japan) and KAL (S Korea). The Chel Ha'Avir purchased its batch of 30 direct from Hughes, and has its own airlift capability for such loads even on trans-atlantic deliveries. The type is the 500MD/TOW, with the Hughes TOW anti-armour missile system sighted by a large stabilized telescopic and all-

IAI Lavi

Lavi (Young Lion)

Origin: Israel Aircraft Industries, Lod Airport.
Type: Multi-role fighter and attack.
Engine: One Pratt & Whitney PW1120 augmented turbojet rated at 12,900lb (5850kg) dry and 20,600lb (9344kg) with maximum afterburner.
Dimensions: Not finalized, but span in neighbourhood of 26ft (8m) and length around 50ft (15m).
Weights: Empty, about 15,000lb (6800kg); loaded (interceptor) about 25,000lb (11,340kg); max (attack or ferry) about 32,000lb (14,500kg).
Performance: Generally similar to F-16.
Armament: Internal gun; probably at least seven hardpoints for external stores to total mass of some 10,000lb (4535kg).
History: First flight possibly late 1984; production delivery January 1988.

Still closely under wraps at the Chel Ha'Avir aircraft programme office and IAI's design offices at Ben-Gurion Airport, the Lavi is the first combat air-craft to be designed in Israel. It is intended to replace the A-4, F-4 and Kfir from about 1992. A very great gamble was taken in choosing the PW1120 engine, because though this uses the HP core of the well-proven F100 the rest of the engine is new and will need prolonged development, without any US government backing. The engine may run at about the time this book appears, but there is no chance of Bet Shemesh and the Bedek Engine Division beginning engine production under licence within 18 months of the 1981 Paris airshow, as was then announced. If a production PW1120 from any source is available by 1986 that will be good timing. The Lavi itself will have a rear-mounted delta wing and fully controllable canard foreplane, with relatively small areas optimized to the lo-level attack mission. Excellent combat manoeuvrability will result from the canard geometry and sophisti-cated variable wing camber and other features, the flight-control system being of the digital fly-by-wire type, presumably without manual reversion. There will be extensive composite primary, as well as secondary, structure,

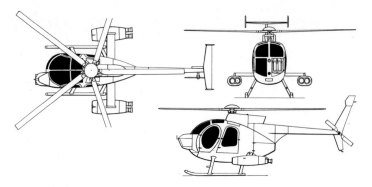

Above: Three-view of 500MD with original exhaust system.

weather sensing sight on the left side of the nose, the pilot being on the right. It is possible that vulnerability of the Israeli force may be reduced by retrofitting with the much more sensible MMS (mast-mounted sight) which enables the helicopter to stay "hull down" below the horizon, a vital factor in survivability in desert areas. They are well equipped with avionics, including 360° radar warning, and have Black Hole Ocarina infra-red suppressing engine exhausts.

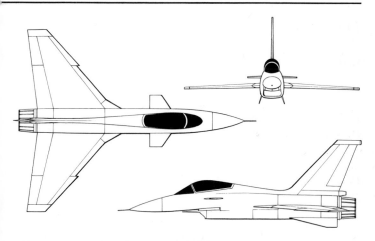

Above: This provisional drawing is based upon an official artist's impression. The spelling is sometimes "Lavie".

while Elta will provide the multi-mode pulse-doppler radar. Four prototypes were planned in 1982, the first to appear in late 1983 (impossible, unless another engine is fitted) and manufacture from production tooling being expected to begin in the late 1980s. By the time this book appears the Lavi may be part of an international programme, in view of the development cost of some $1·2 billion. Indeed Northrop claims the figure will be nearer $2 billion, and is trying to get its F-18L chosen instead. Because of the cost, the programme was suspended in late 1981, but was allowed to go ahead again in February 1982 after a government review. The obvious partner, Saab (with the Model 2105 JAS) of Sweden, has gone too far with its own slightly smaller aircraft, with Swedish-built GE F404J engine. Unofficial Israeli sources tip McDonnell Douglas as the most likely partner, an American company being preferred for political reasons.

RPVs

Israel has an obvious need for remotely piloted vehicles for numerous tactical and other missions. Several types have been produced, two of which have been publicly disclosed.

IAI Scout

Origin: Israel Aircraft Industries, Lod Airport.
Type: Ultralight low-speed RPV.
Engine: One 18hp two-cylinder opposed (fuel/oil mix).
Dimensions: Span 11ft 9¾in (3·6m); length 12ft 1in (3·68m).
Weights: Mission equipment 50lb (22·7kg); fuel 32lb (14·5kg); loaded 260lb (118kg).
Performance: Maximum speed 92mph (148km/h); max-range speed 63mph (101km/h); max altitude 10,000ft (3km); endurance over 4h.

Of twin-boom pusher layout, this simple yet carefully engineered RPV has a small signature and can carry several payloads, chief of which is a tele-photo-lens TV camera servo-pointed on a stabilized mount in a large transparent bubble under the fuselage. A panoramic optical camera can scan 60° each side of the flight path. Normal launch is by catapult, with net retrieval, but tricycle landing gear can be fitted for conventional airfield operation.

Tadiran Mastiff

Mk 1, Mk 2

Origin: Tadiran Electronic Industries, Tel-Aviv.
Type: Multi-sensor ultralight RPV.
Engine: One 14hp Kolbo Korp two-cylinder opposed (Mk 1 tractor, Mk 2 pusher).
Dimensions: Span 14ft 1¼in (4·3m); length 8ft 6¼in (2·6m); height 3ft 3¼in (1·0m); wing area 21·53sq ft (2·0m²).
Weights: Empty 114·6lb (52kg); loaded 165lb (75kg).

Below: Mastiff Mk 2; Tadiran claims that this has more combat-operational hours than any other mini-RPV in the world.

Above: By keeping their objectives modest IAI have produced a field-operational mini-RPV quickly and for a low budget. This Scout is the regular type designed for retrieval in a net.

Performance: Maximum speed 81mph (130km/h); operating speed range 46–69mph (74–111km/h); max altitude 10,000ft (3km); range (fixed ground station) 62 miles (100km), (portable ground station) 124 miles (200km); endurance over 4h.

Extremely similar in most respects to the Scout, the Mastiff was first produced with conventional tractor layout but is now used mainly in pusher Mk 2 form with twin booms to a single-fin tail. Fired pneumatically from a truck-mounted launcher, it carries two TV cameras, various EW and ECM packages and additional options such as a FLIR (forward-looking infra-red) or laser designator. Other versions are tactical missiles with warheads, while a common role is to simulate larger aircraft electronic signatures.

Below: The normal method of getting Mastiff Mk 2 into the air is to accelerate it under air-pressure along a truck-mounted ramp.

Weapons

Guns: Among the hodge-podge of guns in the pre-1956 era, the following were used operationally: Browning machine gun in 0·30in (7·62mm), 0·303in (7·7mm) and 0·5in (12·7mm) calibres; Hispano Mk I, Mk I*, Mk III and Mk V (short and long barrel) all in 20mm (0·787in) calibre; Mauser MG 131 of 13mm (0·5118in) calibre; Mauser MG 151 of 20mm (0·787in) calibre; and new French Hispano 404 of 20mm calibre and DEFA 551 of 30mm calibre. Since 1956 the guns used in Chel Ha'Avir aircraft have been: DEFA 5–52, 5–52A and 5–53 of 30mm calibre (a slightly modified 5–53 being manufactured in Israel); Hughes Mk 11 Mod 5 of 20mm (twin barrel), both alone and in the Mk 4 external pod in some A-4Es and possibly other types (pod cleared for use from OV-1 but not used in Israel); and the 20mm six-barrel General Electric M61A-1 in different installations in the F-4E, F-15 and F-16. For a decade the Chel Ha'Avir has sought to deploy a modern rapid-fire gun of 30mm calibre; while the established DEFA has been evaluated in the F-4E several additional guns have been studied and evaluated, particularly including the General Electric three-barrel XM188.

Unguided missiles: At least 45 types of unguided rocket and bomb have been used by the Chel Ha'Avir, not including a profusion of crude home-made bombs in 1948. At first various British and German bombs and rockets were used, followed from 1950 until 1965 by mainly French types including all standard SAMP bombs and all types of SNEB 68mm rocket. Israel was the original development partner with French industry (Matra, Thomson-Brandt and SAMP) for the so-called "concrete dibber" which made numerous Arab runways unusable during the Six-Day War in 1967; from this weapon Matra developed today's commercially marketed Durandal. Today Israel is self-sufficient with rockets and bombs, most of US design.

Guided missiles: The first guided missile in service was the Matra R 530, two batches of which were purchased along with the Mirage IIICJ and delivered in 1963 and 1965. They proved costly and relatively ineffective and biased the Chel Ha'Avir against such weapons. Nevertheless, with the F-4E a number of AIM-9B Sidewinder and AIM-7E Sparrow AAMs

were acquired, and the Sidewinder at once proved fairly effective. This led to the indigenous development by Rafael Armament Development Authority of the Shafrir (Dragonfly), with better IR homing than AIM-9B and said to be produced for about one-quarter the price. The original production Shafrir was judged the best of all AAMs used in the 1973 war, and since then improved variants have been produced (and exported). As a back-up small purchases have been made of Sidewinder AIM-9J and AIM-9L for use on the F-15 and F-16, but Shafrir Mk 3 or Python 3 is expected to be the standard close-range AAM in 1983–90. It has not been announced whether the Chel Ha'Avir will use a later medium-range AAM such as Sky Flash or AIM-7M. The first ASM (air/surface missile) was the French Nord AS 30, fired from Super Mystère and Mirage aircraft in the Six-Day War. (They were said to have infra-red homing, but in fact the IR system was merely to assist the radio command operator to track these primitive missiles.) All subsequent ASMs appear to have been American, apart from the small wire-guided AS 11 used on Alouette II and possibly other helicopters. Numerically the chief tactical missile is probably AGM-65A Maverick, a 462lb (209·5kg) precision missile with TV guidance. In the 1970s the main precision weapon was probably Walleye, a free-fall missile with a large (825lb, 374kg) warhead and again with TV guidance. The Paveway family of laser-guided "smart bombs" do not appear to have been used, despite their prodigious numbers and wide usage, but the Chel Ha'Avir certainly uses the similar Hobos (homing bomb system) family with EO (electro-optical) guidance driving control surfaces at the rear. The US also supplied several sub-types of AGM-45 Shrike anti-radar missile, virtually all tuned to 2965/2990 and 3025/3050 MHz frequencies to defeat the SA-2 missile; in the 1973 war they were naturally ineffective against the SA-6 (which has CW, continuous-wave, guidance) and in 1974 modification kits were supplied, together with Shrikes of later series tailored to the SA-6. Meanwhile, Rafael began in about 1960 to develop a tactical army missile named Luz which entered service in 1962. From this 12·5-mile (20km) range weapon the Gabriel naval missile was developed. In recent years there have been reports of an air-to-surface missile named Luz-1 but this does not exist despite the publication of such details as TV guidance and a warhead said to weigh 441lb (200kg), and to be able to take out a SAM launcher from a stand-off distance of 50 miles (80km).

Left: The impressive array of stores that can be carried (not all at once) by a Kfir-C2. The largest bomb is the M118 (nominal 3,000lb, 1361kg). Some do not appear to have been publicly identified, and of course Israel has not said a word about its oft-published supposed possession of nuclear bombs – a highly sensitive area.

Below: Mirage and Kfir were the first fighters with Shafrir.

OTHER SUPER-VALUE MILITARY GUIDES IN THIS SERIES......

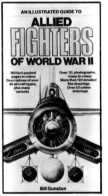

OTHER ILLUSTRATED MILITARY GUIDES NOW AVAILABLE....

Bombers of World War II

German, Italian and Japanese Fighters of World War II

Modern Soviet Navy

Modern Submarines

Modern Tanks

Modern US Navy

Modern Warships

Pistols and Revolvers

Rifles and Sub-Machine Guns

World War II Tanks

* Each has 160 fact-filled pages
* Each is colourfully illustrated with hundreds of action photographs and technical drawings
* Each contains concisely presented data and accurate descriptions of major international weapons
* Each represents tremendous value

Further titles in this series are in preparation

Your military library will be incomplete without them.

PRINTED IN BELGIUM BY

proost
INTERNATIONAL BOOK PRODUCTION